ON MY WAY

BY
CECIL H. PARSONS

Edited by Joyce Hillier-Pritchett

ACKNOWLEDGEMENTS

The author acknowledges with gratitude:

(1) the editorial work done by Joyce Hillier-Pritchett as well as her overall support and encouragement given to me and the project generally. Joyce has been more than an editor. She has been my collaborator, having taken my manuscript and, with great skill and patience, reorganized much of it and rewrote other parts.

(2) permission granted from
   (a) Queen Elizabeth High School and the Eastern School District for the use of the school yearbooks.
   (b) Rebecca George and family for the use of an excerpt of her husband's (Frank George) diary.
   (c) James Combden for the use of his poetry. Jim has enriched my life as well as my manuscript.
   (d) Netta Baker for the songs from her late husband, Jack's compilation.
   (e) the many former students and teachers of Queen Elizabeth High for the use of their works and/or quotes.

(3) partial 'read through' for content by George Evans, Heber Best, Montford Pritchett, Philip Field, Azariah Oram, and our daughter Debra.

(4) typing and copying of manuscript as well as general support by Shirley, my wife.

(5) the use of the following references:
   (a) *Looking Out* by Lloyd Rowsell
   (b) *Memories of Flat Islands* (Reunion Celebrations 1992)
   (c) tape interview of Mr. John Chaytor by Audrey Samson, re the visit of the battleship, the *Cornwall*, connected with the moonshine story on Flat Island. Tape was furnished to me by Audrey. Mr. Chaytor was a native of Flat Island and a fisherman at the time of the incident.
   (d) *NTA Journal* (1957)
   (e) *Cap and Gown* (MUN, 1961)

(6) the article. *The Labrador Connection*, written by Roland Thoms

(7) cover design and other photography done by Cyril Boone

(8) information gained from Sam Saunders who helped me with my Flat Island memories

(9) information shared with me by Scott Crocker at Holy Spirit High School, as well as Wayne Rogers, Michelle Clements and Derek Stevenson at Queen Elizabeth High, re the youth.

Parsons C
18 Cherrington Pl.
Conception Bay South, NL A1W 3A9

ISBN 0-9731851

Printed in Canada by Transcontinental

DEDICATION

To

My Wife & Best Friend,

Shirley

Table of Contents

CHAPTER 1

The Halls of Learning

As I ascend the steps leading to the halls of Memorial University on Parade Street, I am awed by its enormous size. A plaque depicts that it was built as a monument to those who died in the great wars. The University motto stands out boldly, 'PROVEHITO IN ALTUM' - 'Launch Forth into the Deep.' There is no mistake; I am definitely in the right building.

On entering the corridors of this massive structure, I see professors scurrying from one room to another, from one section to another. Each official is wearing a long black gown indicative of the Memorial that the building represents.

And then I meet some people I know – people who attended summer school with me, and are here to take on a year of studies in these great halls. We move through registration, depending on ones faculty. In my case it's Education and Teacher Training. Others are in Engineering, the Sciences, the Arts, etc.

Someone points out a distinguished gentleman moving through the corridor. He is the President of the University, Dr. Raymond Gushue. Later we get to meet him. Our Dean of Education, Dr. George Hickman, is a little guy, but one can see he's in charge.

And so, as the first day ends, some confusion still lingers as we try to sort out our courses, our professors, our classrooms and the complexity of it all. I go back to my boarding house on Bond Street with a lot of apprehension, but, at the same time, feeling honoured to be a part of this process.

This morning I am sitting in the Lecture Theatre, in composition class, with another fifteen or so students. Three days ago we passed in our compositions to our professor for assessment and marking. Word has it that we are getting them back this morning, and I have an uneasy feeling about the whole thing.

Writing essays has never been one of my strong points. My teachers, back in grade school, used to tell me that I had good ideas but had difficulty getting them down on paper.

Most of us sitting here this morning are from the Education Department and have already been teaching out around the bays with 'C' and 'B' licences in one-, two- and three-room schools. We are becoming more familiar with each other as the days pass, and we also realize that what one has gone through in outport teaching experiences, the other has also.

The door swings open and our professor enters, laden with books and assignments. I know she is aware of our weak backgrounds in English especially those students coming from small communities in the outlying areas around the coast. She lays the load down, adjusts her long black gown, (compulsory to be worn by professors and students alike), finds her centre of gravity with those high heel shoes and extends her eyes upward toward the centre isle, focussing her stare towards the area where I am sitting.

I think to myself, 'Is my composition that bad or is there someone else worse than I?' She adjusts her glasses and speaks slowly but distinctly, "I have selected two essays from the group as models for scrutiny and assessment. One is to be used as a good model, the other, a bad model. Hopefully, however, we can learn something from both."

So my mouth is getting dry and I'm hiding partially behind Selby who is broader than I. She continues, "I am going to use the bad model first." She takes the first paragraph and reads verbatim. And now I think it's my composition with all its shortcomings. "Note that run-on sentence and the lack of proper punctuation. Is there any continuity between the third poorly constructed paragraph and the fourth chopped-off one? Ah my! A classic example of bad English." And she reads the second paragraph and the third.

"Get a load of these two dangling participles, and, as well, the adjective, wonderful, is overused." Her eyes are now clearly focussed on me and I wonder when she is going to name names. She begins to pass out the assignments; the one she is reading from is not mine, but I'm included in the five names, called to follow her to her office for further instruction.

About fifteen of us are seated in our Latin 10 class waiting for Mrs. Cochrane to arrive. We are chatting momentarily to those next to us about our backgrounds. Vallis is seated next to me on one side, and Pevie is on the other. They both came from small schools where no Latin was taught. I think I'm pretty lucky because at least I have some beginning background.

One person speaks about the growing size of this fine university and the diversification of its program. Word has it that the registered student population this year is little better than four hundred and fifty. Whow! What a crowd! "And there seems to be a lot more males than females," John remarked, "which is unfortunate for us." Our laughter permeates the corridor, over that statement.

Our professor arrives and apologizes for her lateness. I think to myself, 'Here's a gentle motherly human being, one I'm sure can win the hearts of all those entrusted to her care.' She informs us that this is a non-credit course, a shorter version of high school Latin, to instill in us a basic foundation for Latin 100 in our next step of the Classic Language world.

I can't wait for the Latin classes to roll around. Mrs. Cochrane is as much of a mother to us as she is an instructor. She keeps a close check on our well-being and we enjoy the attention. I am looking forward to Latin 100 in another year because I have to go out teaching to make some money in order to return the following year. I know this is not unusual because many of the education and teacher training students are doing the same thing.

Most students in their first year of university are expected to take certain non-credit courses. Since music is out of my league I selected Art, one period a week. About the only thing that I can draw, so far, is a stick man.

Students in teacher training are expected to take a non-credit course in religious studies, depending on one's denomination. My lot has fallen to the church history of the Church of England.

The most interesting course is the Physical Education under the direction of Mr. Doug Eaton. Here's a man who takes great delight in dealing with those from the bays, and the out harbour areas. His lightheartedness and fine sense of humour help us to relax as we attempt to throw a basketball or volleyball (many of us for the first time). If Mr. Eaton had classes in cock-shots (throwing rocks at a tin can to knock it off) I might come out at the head of the class. Push-ups are not too bad but one still has to align ones arse with ones shoulders. "Keep that rear down," says he, "keep it down."

Courses in Psychology of Education, Methods of High School, and the various discipline approaches, all seem to be interrelated, with each professor taking a personal interest in our training and well-being.

Meanwhile back in our boarding house on Bond Street our boarding mistress, Mrs. Garland, has taken a personal interest in our well-being, especially our church going. Most all the students staying at Mrs. Garlands are of the Anglican denomination and they are her boys as she calls them. When we sit around the table for supper meal she usually stands by the corner and informs us when the church services are at the 'Mother Church' – the Anglican Cathedral. Even though most of us attend the services at the Cathedral she will come and relate to us the total picture – who preached, who did the communion, and what hymns were sung. A fine lady, for sure.

The year slips by all too quickly, and now we are challenged with examinations that test a full year of learning on how to become better teachers. For those of us who have frequented the Nickel Theatre, or spent too much time chasing the fairer sex, it's a bit late to feel regrets.

A Letter From Home

My Dear Son Cecil.

I hope you are keeping well and not working too hard. Your father is getting his salmon nets ready to get to his prime berth at Man Point. Ron and Tootsie have their first child, and they have called her Wavey; and Wilson and Myrtle have their first child, and they have called her Maisie.

The boys are busy now getting ready for the lobster season. Your father and I are well.

> *Love you a lot,*
> *Mom*

About every three weeks I've been getting a letter from my mother. She writes heart-warming news about the family and what is happening back in the Tickle, and she most always has a bit of money tucked inside. 'God bless her,' I think to myself, 'what a lucky guy I am to have a good mom like this.'

I feel privileged to be working with Harvey and Co. for the summer months. The pay cheque is not that great but there are added features that lend prestige to the job. I am stationed in a office on 'pier one' near the waterfront in St John's where great ships are coming and going and unloading their cargo. It is our responsibility, in the checking office, to scrutinize 'bills of lading' and to keep the head office posted of any discrepancies that may occur as well as maintaining normal practices and procedures of transactions.

Of course, it isn't all serious work. I am privileged to be working, side by side, with Tommy and Steve, two well seasoned and knowledgeable veterans of the trade. As well, Max Haynes, a young man of my own age, is also a full time employee, and a great hockey player, in season. We are never stuck for discussion topics which quite often turn into heated debate. Of course, there is always one eye alerted for the approaching head office supervisor who could walk in on us at any time.

The summer flies by all too quickly when one is working full time. I am also painting the big city with a lovely lady, Shirley Clarke, who hails from Carbonear. She tells me she is a member of the AYPA (Anglican Young People Association) and a Sunday school teacher at the Cathedral Hall. She also works at the Royal Stores which is located in the east end on Water Street. She has taken me out to Carbonear for a couple of weekends to visit her mother and two younger sisters, Charlotte and Sybil. Shirley's mom is a fine lady and a great hostess. Her house is one of grandeur, but I'm more intrigued with her beautiful flower gardens. They are a sight to behold. Shirley's father was killed in an industrial accident in Toronto in 1949, the same day Newfoundland joined Confederation. A sad story, indeed.

I have to get back to the Tickle to see my folks before I proceed to Lewisporte where I have accepted a teaching position for the coming year. That's not a problem, but strong ties with the young lady have emerged. My girlfriend and I have developed such a close relationship that we don't know how we are going to get along without each other. When I purchase the engagement ring, Mr. Hawker, the businessman, in Carbonear exclaims that the cost must be equal to a 'winter's grub.' The price, however, seems to be worth the investment.

Shirley's Parents -
Linda and James Clarke

CHAPTER 2

Lewisporte

Protestant amalgamation is in the process at the Central High School in Lewisporte. Four Anglican teachers, including myself, and one Salvation Army, Mr. Arthur Welsh, who is the Vice-Principal, are on the staff. The majority of the staff members are of the United Church faith, with Mr. William Mouland as Principal, a fine man and a great educator.

I have already settled into my boarding house with Mr. and Mrs. Roy Strong on Pleasant Street. They are the salt of the earth and they treat me like one of their own family.

Lewisporte is becoming the hub of the bay. It is obviously a growth area with many people moving in from the outlying areas such as Joe Batts Arm, Fogo, Exploits, Little Bay Islands, Indian Islands and many other places.

The branch railway leading from the Junction, connects with the coastal and passenger boats doing their services around the bay. Employment is increasing around the public wharf; businesses like the central stores, are beginning to spring up; taxis are on the corners; and a hub of activity is taking place.

As I look over my register list I see such names as the Woolfreys, the Manuels, the Collins, the Martins, the Bretts, the Freakes, and others. The school is overflowing and I have to go to the Town Hall for one of my classes. Mr. Penney is in charge of the small school in the East end.

A fine group of children indeed! Well-mannered. The seasoned teachers on the staff have made the newcomers feel at home.

It is now the end of the Thanksgiving weekend and I'm on the train heading back from Carbonear to Lewisporte. The coach where I am sitting is alive with humanity. Suitcases seem to be everywhere. It seems we have taken on a number of lumber-jacks at different stations along the way. Some are wearing brigs and logans and look like very able-bodied men. I have overheard conversations about the woods and 'going up on the line.' I'm familiar with these terms because when I go to the Tickle I hear my two brothers talk about the same thing. Some are going up on the Bishop's Falls Line with Amos Feaner; someone else mentioned George White's Camp, and he thinks Mr. White's camp has the best wood for cutting. One guy has a chew of tobaccy in his mouth; he can barely turn it over, and frequently he has to leave and go out on the landing (where one coach is hooked to another) to squirt the tobaccy juice into the night. Another guy seems to have a tick because his head jerks to one side every now and then. Just a moment, that's not an involuntary movement of his head, he is beckoning to his buddy to go with him to the landing. He seems to have something in his pocket that he wants to share with him. Ah, yes, there is a protrusion inside his jacket, probably a flask with a 'drop of stuff' in it.

I take my walk through the coaches and things are warming up quite nicely. There is the odd piece of music playing and a sing-song is on the go. *'I'se the bye that catches the fish'* seems to be taking the

spotlight, but one of the guys wants to sing the *Badger Drive* and
he starts it:

> *There is one class of men in this country*
> *That never is mentioned in song*
> *But now since their trade is advancing*
> *They'll come out on top before long*

He finishes the first verse and encourages others to join in the chorus.

> *With their pike-poles and peavies and bateaus and all*
> *And they're sure to drive out in the spring that's the time*
> *With the caulks in their boots as they get on the logs*
> *And it's hard to get over their time.*

Tin suitcases are laid in the aisles and some people are sitting on
them because there is nowhere else to sit. The train is alive with
excitement. I finally make my way back to my seat and crash. Later
I hear the conductor's voice 'Notre Dame Junction, next station.'
As I prepare to leave the coach I am a little embarrassed because one
lady sitting opposite me informs me that I had my feet in her hat
bag for most of the time while I was sleeping. Alas! A casualty of
exhaustion.

In preparation for the aftermath of the Christmas wedding, I rent
Mr. Combden's house adjoining Mr. Tom Gillingham's, the barber.
My mother and father come in from the Tickle and settle in the
house to help prepare for the bride's homecoming later. Father gets
work as a stevedore on the public wharf until the shipping season
closes.

The marriage takes place in fine style at Carbonear on December 29 with a different approach than it would have been in the Tickle. No powder guns are fired, and no boats are used. There is such a snowstorm that not even the best man could get out from St. John's. We wouldn't dare postpone the ceremony because of the threat of bad luck, according to the elders.

Shirley is escorted up the aisle by her two grandfathers, one on either side. The ceremony is performed by Rev. W.H.B. Gill who also christened me back in the 'Tickle.'

After the reception at the hall, we get a little more into the party mood at the house. Mrs. Clarke, Shirley's mom, welcomes me and emphasizes that it is good to have a son in the family. Mrs. Sinyard, Shirley's grandmother, who had already lent me her belt off her dress, prior to the marriage ceremony, to help keep up my trousers, since I had misplaced mine, now wants it back even if my pants do fall down. I seem to be joining one big happy family. On one occasion, both grandfathers approach me. Grandfather Clarke, a very mild-mannered person, lays his hand on my shoulder and says, "Son, I know you're going to treat her right and look after her." Grandfather Sinyard, the Viking of the extended family, digs me in

Shirley's Grandparents - Martha and Corbett Sinyard, and Luke Clarke picnicing on Heart's Content Barrens. (circum 1951)

the ribs with his iron fist and exclaims, "Sonny, you better take care of her or you'll have to deal with me." And then he goes back for another round while I try to ease the pain afforded me by his supposed affectionate pat.

Back in Lewisporte a second reception is waiting with friends. A staff party is held for us at the school at which time Marcia sings the little ditty, 'She went into the water and she finally got it wet.'

The winter, with its blankets of snow and natural ice bridge across the arm, is slipping by quickly. On Saturdays father and I skate across the harbour to the opposite side where we cut firewood and portage (carry) it across the ice on our catamaran (slide). It's like old times again, bringing the Tickle to Lewisporte. It is also a healthy and enjoyable activity after interacting with so many students on a daily basis.

At home I'm aware there's a strong bond developing between my wife and my mother. Mother is teaching Shirley how to cook fisherman's brewis so that the brewis won't turn out soggy. 'Bring the brewis to a boil, my dear, but don't let it boil.' Pork fat and scrunchions are a delicacy. Shirley has her special dishes to which mother becomes partial.

Father has been entertaining me with his stories of long ago – stories of which I never grow tired. He tells me he was twelve years old when he took the old musket – the long gun, out of the house, unnoticed to Grandma Susie, and killed his first seal, a jar (a bay seal). All the men were gone on the Labrador fishing at the time. He told me about the time a man perished in the snow storm. He was walking from Point Leamington to Thimble Tickles and got caught in a blinding snow blizzard. Uncle Arthur Haggett found him kneeling up to a tree. He said he was close to the half-way camp but just missed it. A sad story indeed!

He told me about the family, over in Green Bay, who actually starved to death during the depression. My father gave a great sigh, "Cecil, my son, it was tough back then during the depression and I hope to God we will never have to return to those days again."

"Come on, father," I say, "let's get a cup of tea."

"A good strong one," says he, "not a drop of slops."

Like I said earlier, the town of Lewisporte is growing by leaps and bounds. New houses are being built, and a number of new businesses have opened. I had occasion to meet the Mayor of the Town, Mr. Walter Woolfrey, who, with the other members of the Council, are doing a fine job.

Our school, the Central high School, is full to capacity. I find a great deal of satisfaction teaching here; the teachers seem to be one big family with support coming from all directions - the parents, the clergy and the business community.

Shirley is working with Mr. Scott Woolfrey in his store. She is also involved with the church and teaching Sunday school. She relates one amusing incident, "I was checking to see how well some of them knew the commandments; so I asked one boy to recite the eighth commandment and as quick as you can wink your eye he had it, 'Thou shall not swipe, Miss.'

Even though Calvin Coates is the main lay reader in the Anglican Church, under the direction of Rev. Reuben King, I sometimes get the occasional spot to help. Mr Fred Earle is outstanding as an organist in the Church.

Tonight the four of us are sitting around the table having a snack before bed-time. Mother looks at me and she says, "I know teaching school today is not like when I went to school." And she tells

about it. "Shirley, my dear, I lived on Burnt Island and we had a little school there. There was one on Cull's Island, one on the South
Side and one up in Marshs' Arm. Of course Mr. Snow, the dear
man, always called it Winter House Cove which was the correct
name. They were all one-room schools. We could only go for a half
a day, and that was for only about three months a year. The next
three months, the school master spent up in the Arm (Winter
House Cove). The schoolmaster would move around – two or
three months here and a couple of months there. Treffie Chippett,
that's Aunt Triffie Snow you know her as, taught school on Burnt
Island for a while. One of the teachers, we used to call him the
school master, was Mr. Leander Rowsell. I went to school to him,
and sometimes some of us would get in the boat with him and go
to the South side to school. Cecil, you always called him Uncle
Leander. You know the man that was retired and lived just down
from us."

I nod my head that I remember.

"He was a strict teacher but a good one. He spent a lot of time on
the Labrador teaching before I went to him. Of course, he
belonged to the Tickle in the first place."

My father joins in the conversation, "Well, Cecil, I think we told
you before that Uncle Leander spent a number of years down on
the Labrador; it was during the First World War years and shortly
after. It was down around Battle Harbour and Sandwich Bay, that
area. He used to tell me about it; he said it was so cold in the winter that he had to wear two suits of fleece-lined underwear, one on
top of the other to keep warm."

My mother gets to speak again "Yes, my dear, he did a lot of good
for the people down there, travelling from one place to another by
dog team in the winter and by boat in the summer. He was trained
at Queens College and was called a Mission or Church Teacher.

My dear, he had permission from the Bishop to marry people and give the Holy Communion. He suffered a lot of hardship in those years. A good man, my dear, a good man."

Father speaks, "Yes, Cecil, my son, there were a number of good school masters back then, and now, too, of course; but back then they had to keep the prayers in church and do the Sunday school. If there was a special letter to be written, a paper to be filled out or some important thing, the Master was called on to do it. Very few people in the Tickle, and I'm sure in other places, had enough learning to do it right. A fine man for sure was Uncle Leander."

After spending a pleasant year at Lewisporte, we move back to the Tickle for the summer and some relaxation in the fishing boat.

Shirley is somewhat excited, but at the same time a little apprehensive, about meeting all those new people in the Tickle.

The second day she is there Uncle Henry Parsons takes her out in his motor boat and steams around the Tickle explaining its lay-out and how it got its name. He explains the various Tickles – Western, Eastern, Northern – and how they all lead into Leading Tickles. He tell her about The Ladle, a very narrow channel of water, that separates the mainland from Cull's Island, and through which the *Clyde*, the coastal boat, goes through, sometimes scraping her keel, at low tide.

And then she said he went into the island names and the first inhabitants – Rowsells, Chippetts, Haggetts, Noseworthys, Parsons, Guys, Earles, Alcocks. Shirley is certainly getting initiated to the customs of the Tickle. Uncle Eli Haggett died a couple of days ago, and, during his funeral which Shirley attended, one of the elders approached her and attempted to pin a black band on her arm indicating her relationship through marriage (my father calls it 'fork relation'). I don't think Shirley was impressed.

As for me I'm enjoying myself out cod fishing with father. We use the trawl and, as well, we use the hook and line. Some mornings we find ourselves out on deepwater bank and Uncle Israel's spot, with the grapnel down, watching the sun rise, while sizing our lines as the fish tug and lurch. Bladders are beginning to form on the teacher's hands, and father exclaims, "How nich is your hands atol."

Father continues to yarn and tell me stories of days gone by as we fill our mid-ship room with fine cod that wrestle for resting places among the fish already settled.

This morning he is looking in at Burnt Island and smiling to himself. I say, "Dad, what's funny?" After some hesitation he responds, "You know, Cecil, I was thinking about when I used to court your mother. She lived on Burnt Island and I lived on Rowsell's Island. I used to take the punt and row across Burnt Island Tickle. In the spring of the year when the slob ice blocked my way I would row up on the back of Rowsell's Island and go to Man Point Cove. Your mother would walk from Burnt Island Cove across the neck to Man Point Cove and help me pull in the punt".

I ask, "How would she know when you were coming?"

He laughs, "We had our signs; she never missed."

I think to myself, 'What a beautiful love story.'

And now I'm scoating (hauling), as Wilson would say, on another big fish. By the way, we can see Wilson and Dummy Gill on their trawl up off Don-neir.

Arch Ward is head of the local roads committee here in the Tickle this summer. He offered me a job, working on the local roads, using the pick and shovel. The pay is $5 for one day, the second day one has to work for free. I think I'll stick with the hook and line and the summer on the sea – a most healthy environment.

CHAPTER 3

Flat Island

So tonight I'm listening to the Gerald S. Doyle Bulletin and the message comes over the wire, 'Wanted a Principal for the two-room school at Flat Island, Bonavista Bay.' I will send a telegram tomorrow, applying for the position.

The message I receive from the chairman of the board on Flat Island reads, "The board accepts your application. Please confirm."

As the passenger boat docks at the wharf on Flat Island, we are greeted by the chairman, Mr. Bill Samson. While we are disembarking he asks two questions of me: 'Parsons, will you lay-read in the church? Where did you get her?' The latter question referring to my lovely lady.

The Principal's residence is spacious and has a wood and coal burning stove. I'm notified that all the coal will be paid for by the church in return for my lay-reading and other church duties. I am also informed that the square of ground, where potatoes are set and growing, out in front of the residence, belongs to the teacher. Apparently the teacher, each year, regardless of whether he is returning or not, sets the potato seeds. The residents look after the trenching and weeding if the teacher is not there, throughout the summer.

We do have an immediate problem, however. Our bit of furniture is on the coastal steamer, in route. "Don't worry," they say. The

The teacher digging potatoes on Flat Island - 1955

chairman of the board and his wife extend their hospitality for us to stay as long as we wish. Mr. and Mrs. Isaac Decker supply us with a bed for the residence, and Neville and Tricksy Ralph become our very close friends.

The school teacher bringing water at the residence on Flat Island

As I look over my charges, I'm awe-struck by the maturity and enthusiasm of those students. They just seem to want to get on with it. All I need to do is point the way. I am looking at my list now and I see Albert Ralph, and Marina Samson, two mature students. I see the names of Weldon Ralph, Scott Blake, Tom Cheater, Jim Morgan, Charlie Hiscock, Ralph Moss, John Butt, Christine and Carol Samson, and the list goes on.

I am told that Mr. Newton Morgan who preceded me as Principal, did a fine job of keeping them on their toes, and promoted the cause of education.

This is, indeed, a year to remember – a year filled with support from all sides. The students are remarkable in their maturity, their work habits, and their respectability for me and my position. If I make a mistake in reference or give an incorrect response one of them will set me straight but not during class but after they have been dismissed.

The residence is always open at night to students having academic problems; the odd one will find his way along and we will work things out saving precious time tomorrow for new beginnings.

The parents and the people in general are unique in their desire for education for their children, which seems to be the number one priority. If a student ever dreams of getting out of hand and the parents get wind of it, it is nipped in the bud immediately.

Every Sunday morning and evening I don the cassock and gown and lead in the church services. The great St. Nicholas Church rings out with some fine hymn singing. They flock to worship in mass and find hope for the future and fellowship in their togetherness.

Occasionally the minister from Salvage, puts in an appearance and administers the sacrament of communion. On one occasion during the lenten season my wife and her friend met the Reverend on the road. After an exchange greeting he indicated he had given up smoking cigarettes for the forty days but he is puffing away on a fine crooked stem pipe. Shirley's friend, I feel certain was thinking out loud when she exclaimed, "Parson, I call that trying to fool the devil in the dark."

The state of the economy is like no other that I have witnessed up to this point. Those who are not employed in some form on the island, are off some where else making a living. Every family seems to have full and plenty. A remarkable state of well-being!

There has been a number of 'times' (hot suppers and dances) throughout the year – all good I might add, whether done by the CEWA (Church of England Women Association) or THE LODGE or any other group. A square dance or reel usually follows the meal, and there doesn't seem to be a problem getting dancers. Their dances are similar to those of the Tickle with one variation. Toward the end of the dance they'll sometimes position the fiddler in the centre of the sixteen-handed dance and dance around him.

There is also a practice here among some men to go house to house on special occasions, extending good will and sampling each ones 'drop of stuff.' Tonight I'm asked to accompany them. When we arrive at my bachelor friend's house, his parents are already retired for the night. While the others are doing their sampling Wes, my bachelor friend, invites me up the stairs to meet his aging parents.

When I arrive at the room they are sitting up in bed, waiting. Wes introduces me and we exchange greetings. Then the skipper directs Wes to go to the clothes closet and get a drop of his good stuff, that he has for special moments. We share a warm moment indeed.

Tonight I'm over to Mr. Aaron Ralph's, where I often go to listen to his delightful yarns. Uncle Aaron, a veteran of the First World War, and a bit of an entertainer, keeps me on the edge of my chair, spell-bound, with his stories about years ago.

Tonight, as well, he looks at me and says, "Parsons, you should join our lodge." So he tells me about the Orange Lodge and what it is all about. "Now, what about it?" says he with his hearty laugh. How can I refuse this man I respect so much?

"Parsons, my man," says he, "we'll be gentle on you in conferring the Orange, and the Blue but the ROYAL Arch..." and then he laughs again. He also tells me that maybe that will be all the degrees they will confer in my school year.

After a six-handed game of auction with Mrs. Ralph, Neville, Trixie, and Shirley we settle back for a fine cup of tea and continue to shoot the breeze. "Parsons," says he, "did you ever hear about the moonshine fiasco that happened right here on Flat Island?"

"Can't say as I did, sir," I replied.

"Well, Parsons, b'y, it happened in 1919 right after the war; I was just back from overseas." So he tells me the story about the police and the Man-of-War ship coming to the island to investigate the rumour that some men were making moonshine.

Says he, "Parsons, my son, our women are not easily scared now but they were less then. But to see the carrier boat coming with a big gun mounted on her was enough to stir your nerves."

We are sitting there sipping on a 'drop of stuff' and I'm straining forward to get every word. "That's quite a story," I say.

"Yes, but the best of it all was the reporter on board the ship. Do you know who he was?" Again I plead ignorance.

"He was Joey Smallwood, our Premier, today. He was called the Barrelman."

And then he laughed with his hearty laugh, and we all joined in with him.

Bert Samson has just gone '30 for 60' on his hand, and Kate tells him that he's bluffing. "Try me," says he. Uncle Gill, that's Bert's father, winks at me and proceeds to lay the board with a whist. It's men against the women, and it's shaping up to be a 'doosie.' Aunt Violet cross-plays with a big one and the tone is set for 'ructions'. With a tie game we leave the 'blood one' for another night.

Uncle Gill is a very jolly individual, and one of the two merchants on the Island. He can sit all night telling yarns. Over the year he has told me a lot about the origin and development of Flat Islands. At one time he said the community boasted of thirty odd schooners and as many as nine hundred residents. Now the population is down to three hundred and on the slide. He tells me about some of the great people that the school on the island had produced – ministers, teachers, nurses, sea captains, and many other vocations as well. He then turns to me quickly, as an afterthought, and excitedly says, "Have you heard the Moonshine Story?"

"I've heard bits and pieces, Mr. Samson, but tell it again."

"Well, I'll tell ya." And with that delightful laugh he proceeds. He is about as far as the stand-off between the police who had their rifles pointed and some of the men on the island gone for their guns, when Aunt Violet beckoned for us to come to the table for a cup of tea. I feel sure we'll get the rest of the story later.

It's Christmas and Garfield and Lucy Butt have invited us over to their home for a scoff. The plan is for the women to 'dress up' to go mummering and when they get back Garfield will have the meal prepared. Lucy dresses as a teddy bear and sits in the middle of the floor to demonstrate her role. No doubt she is a game for any kind of a trick while knocking on the neighbours' doors.

While they are gone Garfield tells me about the big ship, the *Cornwall*, as he heard it told to him. I must say the story varies from one person to another depending who's telling it. So far I've heard the story told by four or five of the residents. Mr John Chaytor is delightful too at telling the story. I'll try to tell the story as I think I understand it.

It was in the spring of 1919 that word got to the government of the day that some of the men on Flat Island were openly 'running off' moonshine – a very potent concoction. The two policemen that were stationed at Greenspond were ordered to proceed to the Island and investigate. The men on the island got wind of this and a number of them took to their boats, intercepted the police before the reached there, and ordered them to turn around and head back or face the possibility of being tossed overboard.

The two policemen went back to their station and telegraphed the Justice Department in St. John's notifying them of their failed attempt to get to the island. More police were sent down and the second time around nine policemen went to the island and landed. When the police positioned their rifles, a few of the men went home and got their guns and there was a stand-off, but no guns were fired. After a while the police withdrew to their boats and left the island.

Again the Department of Justice was telegraphed of the incident by the police. The Minister of Justice, Morine, in the government of Sir Michael Cashin, decided to send the Man-of-War ship, the

Cornwall, that was visiting St. John's at the time, down to the island to deal with the situation. The big ship arrived in Bonavista Bay in June month, picked up the police at Greenspond and headed for the island near which she anchored. When the party arrived on the island in the armed carrier all they saw was a woman standing on the wharf with a baby in her arms waiting for the steamer. What the police didn't know was that most of the men had already boarded their schooners and were on the way to the Labrador for the summer's fishing voyage.

The police entered some homes, did a search and arrested six or seven (depending on who is telling the story) men and carried them to St. John's on board the War Ship and had them placed in the lock-up. According to Mr. John Chaytor some of the men the police wanted were down on the Labrador, fishing from their schooners. So the boat, the *Ingram* was sent down to have them brought up to St. John's. Two skippers and a shareman were taken from their schooners. Later they were returned to their homes and schooners on the Labrador. All of this happened on the eve of an election. There is a political side behind it, but I won't get into that. Needless to say some Flat Islanders tell this story with a twinkle in their eyes and a smile on their faces and amuse themselves at the folly of government officials like Morine in prohibition times.

This year has been, truly, one to remember for a long time. Shirley took charge of the Sunday School for the year. She helped to organize a concert and played her part on stage. One will hardly forget the fine talent that the people displayed on stage. A classic example was Jim Morgan performing *"My father's old Sou'wester."*

The Lodge put me through my ropes as they administered all the degrees, right to the Red Cross, by Good Friday. I was fully aware that they were enjoying putting the 'school master' through.

Memorial University is calling. I have to go.

As the passenger boat makes its way from the island, toward the mainland, I stand on deck and stare back at the place that was home to us for a year – a great year. I feel sad leaving a community of people who are the salt of the earth, who are steadfast in their purpose, and who taught Shirley and me a lot about the purpose of life.

I see Shirley wiping away a tear as we take in the big picture – the dominant white and well kept houses, the outstanding personalities behind the doors, and St. Nicholas Church towering above everything else and dominating the landscape with its spire of ninety feet reaching for the Heavens.

 It is September, 1958 and we are sitting in our kitchen listening to the radio and the commentator says, "We now take you to St. Nicholas Church on Flat Island where four- or five-hundred people

St. Nicholas Church, Flat Island.

have gathered for the last service in this beloved church." The last hymn is sung.

"Thy hand, O God, has guided,
Thy flock from age to age..."

Shirley and I embrace each other and try to empathize with the feelings that we know are dominating those good people gathered in this sanctuary for the last time.

Shirley and I are spending some time at Hearts Content this summer, at the home of her grandparents, Corbett and Martha Sinyard. I have already dubbed Grandfather as a Viking because of his physical appearance – tall, lean with hands of steel. I never tire of listening to him about his travels on the high seas, and the many mysterious experiences of his rugged life.

One experience that stands out is when they were returning in their schooner from the Labrador after being down there all summer fishing. He relates, "Cecil, my son, we was about a day's sail from Hearts Content when a bird, a strange bird, come and pitched on the mast head and wouldn't go away. I kept me eye on it; I got this uneasy feeling, so I said to the skipper, 'Skipper what do you make of that bird?'

He said, 'Corb, bye, that bird got bad news, from back home. Someone is passed on.' When we reached the harbour in Hearts Content, I could see me house in Southern Cove and I noticed the blinds was hauled down. I knowed someone was dead belonging to me. When I looked up to the masthead, the bird was gone after being there all day. Billy, my thirteen-month-old son was dead."

It was during this summer I met one of the great leaders and educators of Hearts Content by the name of Cyril Bull. Mr. Bull has been here for some time as principal of the all grade school. Here is a man the people speak of with affection and respect because of his leading roles, not only as principal and teacher but lay-reader in the Church, Justice of the Peace, a man for all seasons and called on for all reasons.

And then through Mr. Bull, I meet Mr. Lidstone, principal and teacher, one of the pillars of Winterton, as well as Mr. Eldred Warren, principal of Hearts Delight school. One can't help but admire the moral strength and convictions of these teachers who play a vital role in enhancing the well-being of the general population in various places around the coast.

Shirley and I, like a good many more teachers and their families, are living on the edge – the edge of poverty. Granted, many teachers around the island are teaching on licences which constitute a poverty standard – less than $100 a month on B and C licences. I'm a little better than that on a certificate, but not much better.

Both the Department of Education and the Newfoundland Teachers Association are very concerned about the large percentage of poorly qualified teachers, the high percentage leaving the profession and the number of small schools around the coast with no teachers at all. In some cases boards hire people not licenced, to teach in one and two-room schools because they can't find qualified teachers.

We are at a point in our lives when we have to decide whether I'll stay in the profession or go – go back to the Tickle fishing or go into some other vocation. If I stay, I must upgrade, that means spending the meagre amount we have saved.

I have heard it said that 'Teaching is a noble profession.' That may be very true; certainly teachers have to like what they are doing and be dedicated to the cause of imparting sound knowledge to the children entrusted to their care.

I hear that a brief has been worked on by a committee, headed up by Mr. Cliff Andrews, President of N.T.A. (Newfoundland Teachers Association) and Mr. Alan Bishop, Secretary, to put forward some recommendations on teachers' salaries. Word has it that the starting salaries for the top of grade IV could go as high as $3300 a year. That will be an improvement.

I did make a decision to stay in the education profession; so we are settled away in a boarding home in old downtown St. John's. Shirley has been fortunate in getting a job as head of the shoe department in Woolworths new department store on Water Street. She's bringing home, with a lot of overtime, as much money in a week as I made in a month, in my last teaching job.

I am settled in at Memorial Campus on Parade Street for another year. Word has it that the enrollment has surpassed 600. Really growing!

A Letter From Home

My dear son, Cecil:

I received your kind letter and I'm glad that you are both doing well. Your father and I are fine; don't worry about us.

Your father is working on the local roads, and doing fairly well with the fall fish. Seems like everyone who passes his net at Man Point brings salmon to him.

My dear, I got to tell you, Uncle Henry Ward and Dummy Fred are in the General Hospital in St. John's. They both got to have operations. I hope you can get time to visit them. You know what it's like if you don't

see anyone from home. You get lonesome, not knowing what's going on.
I'm sure Uncle Henry doesn't mind so much because he can get along
with anyone. It's Dummy Fred, the poor soul, where he can't talk and
hear and all. He'll be some proud to see you and to sign with you. I
know Ruby Snow will go to see them too. Take care and don't study too
hard.

Love, Mom

I do get down to see Uncle Henry and Dummy Fred. Shirley, however, goes almost every day when she's off work. She tells me
Dummy Fred is up to the window waiting for her to get off the bus.
He tells her the nurses are nice but he can't wait to get back home
and get his arms around Aunt Bertha. Shirley also gives him the
happy news that he has another grandson, Barry, born to Wilson
and his daughter Myrtle.

Both Dummy Fred and Uncle Henry Ward told Shirley they will be
her Guardian Angels after they die. I think it's because they are so
appreciative of the many visits she made to the hospital to see them
and the care packages she has taken to them. They both have had
their surgery and are doing fine.

CHAPTER 4

Carbonear

As one gazes over the landscape from Saddle Hill, one can see a well-kept community, dotted with churches signifying a diversification of religious denominations. Carbonear Island guards the entrance to the waterfront whose north side parallels the busy business establishments along Water Street.

As we settle into the Russell Homestead on Bemister's Hill, I am informed of the goodness and greatness of this fine man, Stephen Russell, who has now gone to his great reward. His wife, who, I'm sure, will be an inspiration to us, lives in the other part of the house.

Mr. Russell spent years teaching the children of St. James School, of which I am now Principal. I feel honored to stand where he once stood – a man of great character, spiritual strength, a principal, teacher, a lay-reader of the church, former mayor (and the first one, I think) of Carbonear, Justice of the Peace – indeed, a man for all the people.

I have succeeded Mr Sam Pittman who is a fine educator, and did a great job here at St. James, according to the folks that know him.

Others teachers on the staff this year are Sonia Wells, Vina Bickford and Doreen Parrott, all caring and concerned people. As I look through the register I see the names of Marilyn Gill, James Green, Fred Rossiter, Ada Green, Cecil Oates, Joyce Earle, Bill Earle,

Winston Thoms, to name a few. My class in the senior room is made up of approximately thirty students in a multi-grade setting. Here we have a fine group of students who are well disciplined in their approach to work habits and have great respect for their teachers. The educational process in grades nine, ten, and eleven is regulated by the Department of Education and the Public Examination guidelines.

A teacher in this type of multi-subject and multi-grade environment has to be prepared for what the next hour is going to present. One becomes very busy with a range of subjects such as Latin, mathematics, social studies, sciences, English at different levels, reaching down into the upper elementary level. There is no such thing as specialization; one has to know a little about all fields.

We have now established a base for learning and we are off to a worth-while beginning.

This is a day to remember and treasure. Shirley and I have just now finished extending hospitality to the Captain and crew of the research boat, the *Sandy Point*. My total experience in the research field warrants a descriptive overview.

While studying at Memorial University this past year, I applied to the Department of Fisheries Research for a summer position. With many thanks to Hubert Squires, a scientist at the Biological Research Station, I was appointed assistant technician and placed under his supervision. My job placed me on the research boat, the *Sandy Point*, researching the availability of scallops along the coast of the province.

After spending three wonderful months with Captain Gordon Harris and his hearty crew, doing sets for scallops, taking water salinity and temperatures, sampling and keeping daily records of procedures, I now reflect on this great experience. Needless to say we had a diversification of experiences and many exciting moments.

One of the incidents I wish to relate was my relationship with Uncle John, a deck hand. I never grew tired of his stories that told of his near-miss experiences, sailing the Atlantic seaboard. He cited one experience when their three-mast schooner swamped (went down into heavy seas and winds), and they were left clinging to the cross trees all night until rescued the following day.

Every day when I prepared my scallop sample, Uncle John would be the one to remove the trap-hatch for me to descend to the hole to store my sample. At one point in time Uncle John was nowhere to be seen when I had my sample ready, so I removed the hatch and placed it bottom up just as Uncle John was reappearing from the companionway of the foscile. His face revealed one of shock and horror.

I said, "Uncle John, what's wrong?"

"Oh, Cec, oh Cecil, my son, what have you done, what have you brought on our heads?"

"Uncle John, what did I do?" Suddenly my father's advice began to dawn on me.

"You know what you have done, Cecil, my boy. You have brought bad luck to this boat, you have jinxed her." And he grabbed the hatch and turned it right side up. Our relationship deteriorated somewhat, needless to say.

One day when we were steaming along the south-west coast toward Francois, the Captain turned to me and said, "Cec, that rock on the chart there about seven knots on course is above the water?" He always asked me to check the chart with him. He was always right, so I glanced without looking and said, "Yes, Skipper."

A half an hour later I heard the vicious oath come from his lips as he abruptly pulled the engine from full speed to reverse and spun the wheel to starboard, as we looked in horror at the rock below water and a disaster that was narrowly averted. Uncle John was shaking his head and pointing an accusing finger at me, reminding me of the curse I had brought on the *Sandy Point*.

I could write a book on the summer's excursions that took us to every nook and corner of the west and south coasts.

Like I say, we entertained the Skipper and the crew of the *Sandy Point*, tied up at the wharf in Carbonear. We reminisced about the summer events – the feed of lobsters at Castor River, the ashore party at Curling, the dance at Piccadilly, the storm that saw us watching the anchor in Cow Head... and the chatter went on...

A fine captain and his crew – the salt of the sea !

Occasionally we go over to the parsonage for a game of cribbage or auction. The Rev. and Mrs. Gill and his aging parents who hail from Pinchard's Island, Bonavista Bay, make up the team.

The Parson tells me stories about his Mission in Exploits, about his Mission boat that took him all the way to Tilt Cove over in Green Bay. Many a time he said his engine would break down and he would find himself drifting out the bay – sometimes in heavy winds and swells. His big Newfoundland dog that accompanied him on all trips was his true companion and a lifeline. I was told back in the Tickle that on one occasion the Parson fell overboard, moving from forward to aft, and the dog rescued him from the cold waters.

He said that most fishermen, fishing along the coast, knew the mission boat by sight and looked out for him.

Later the Rev. Fred Oake, who hailed from Change Islands, took over the Mission of Exploits and followed the same path. Rev. Oake told me he couldn't use the old mission boat that former clergy had; it was too far gone. He requested another and they sent him a life boat that was klinker built. In other words it appeared to be clapboarded and he had a double-cylinder ten horsepower Acadia engine in it. One time he was making his rounds over in Green Bay when he damaged the rudder and was drifting out the bay all night. He did, however, manage to reach a point of land and was able to haul her stern in far enough to fix the problem. The next day the coastal steamer, the *Glencoe*, came looking for him. Those two men of God had one big thing in their favor – they grew up in the fishing boat and knew a great deal about the sea and what to do in times of rough water and storms. When I think of the hardship that many of those clergy and priests went through back in those days to minister to their parishioners and the sick, I can't help but think how indebted we are to them.

Since I came to Carbonear I have met a number of distinguished educators. A well-known and long-time educator, Helen Earle, is teaching in the one room school on the South Side. Helen has been there for quite a number of years and has made a great contribution to the community in general.

Another fine educator, Mr. Hudson Davis, is Principal of the United Church Academy here at Carbonear. I am indebted to Mr. Davis for his help and support in the educational field of endeavour and enlightenment. He made it a point, early in the school year, to come and visit me at St. James and offer any assistance. He, as well, stands out in his service to the Regional Branch of the

Newfoundland Teacher's Association. An outstanding leader in the community and a fine gentleman !

Another fine educator who used to teach at St. James is Beatrice Hawker-Forward. As well, she serves the community well in guiding, and as an organist at St. James Church.

As I said before, we are now living in the Russell Residence, two doors down from the stately house in which Shirley grew up. She tells me the house was filled with lots of spiritual guidance and formalities – family Bible reading and prayers, church going and Sunday rituals, and close and treasured relationships in the extended family.

I feel that I should relate the wonderful father-daughter relationship that dominated the household between Shirley and her dad. From what she tells me they just did things together – the church choir, the on-stage drama, the trouting expeditions. It sounds like a daughter worship for her dad and the good things he stood for.

And then the tragedy – her father James, at the age of thirty-six, was killed in an industrial accident, in Toronto, on the same day that Newfoundland became the tenth Province of Canada. The family was devastated and Shirley was crushed, like many others who had similar experiences. She was marooned in a sea of sadness. Her treasured memories with her father, will be told and retold for years to come.

Shirley tells her most treasured memory of her Dad. "It had to be when I was five years old. Daddy was working with Saunders and Howell. He was sent to Botwood to work on the Armed Forces Base that was being built there. Before he went he asked me what did I wanted Santa to bring me for Christmas and I said a pair of fur-tops. Later, word was that he would not be home for Christmas. Before I went to bed Christmas Eve, Mom asked me what I wanted Santa to bring me and I said, "Bring my Daddy home."

Christmas Eve came and no Daddy. I went to bed feeling sad and lonely, but when I got up in the morning the fur-tops were in my stocking. I knew then that daddy was home."

A Letter From Home

My Dear Son Cecil,

I hope you and Shirley are keeping well. Your father and I are fine. Your father is doing well with the salmon, especially at Man Point. I wish you were here to enjoy some pan fried, and a feed of lobsters.

My Dear, you know Uncle Henry Parsons passed away because Ron sent you a telegram. He died sitting up in his chair reciting his favourite hymn.

Uncle Henry Ward and Uncle Arthur Haggett passed away too.

We still got to go to Compass Cove for a drop of drinking water. My dear, the water is not fit to drink where everybody is going down in the well with their boots on, dipping the brook dry. We call it feet water. Your father takes the barrel aboard the boat and we go to Flat Rocks up in Compass Cove. All you can see in the summer are people with their barrels aboard.

We still go back to Rowsell's Island to set our potato seed in the two big squares of ground and trench them with caplin that are rolling on the beach nearby. Of course I take along the iron bake pot to cook up a feed of salmon or fisherman's brewis. I'm longing for you to get home so that I can get my arms around you again. Oh my! The good times and laughs we used to have. Look after yourself,

Love, Mom

CHAPTER 5

Burgeo

The Newfie Bullet jerks to the left and then to the right as its engines strain to take us over the Gaff Topsails. Shirley and I have settled in our berths, but sleep passes me by as I lie there contemplating the year that lies ahead of us. We are in new territory, heading toward Port Aux Basques where we will join the steamer to take us to our destination – Burgeo. We are both young, healthy and looking to break new ground.

I hear the conductor's voice now, "Corner Brook, next station." We crawl out of our crammed quarters and head for the dining room. We can see the crowds at the station as the train comes to a jerking halt. Some are getting off, while others are lumbering aboard with their bags, boxes and suitcases. There's a lot of hugging and kissing, laughing and crying; the deck is alive with humanity.

We sit at the dining room table enjoying this moment as we watch love, joy and sadness have its fling. "All aboard, all aboard," shouts the conductor, and the Newfie Bullet is on her way. As we approach each station the conductor makes his way through the coaches announcing the next station. Someone is calling him conductor Daniels – a distinguished looking gentleman, indeed.

I have ordered a full breakfast and it tastes delicious. I have to watch my chances with the coffee. I bring it to my mouth but at that moment the train lurches, the mug collides with my nose, and I quickly set it down, waiting for a lull and then quickly bring it back to my mouth again. Shirley is smiling; she has already gotten it right.

Our cribbage game that we started yesterday has reached the 'blood game stage' and we are now concentrating on every move. Once in a while we are pleasantly interrupted by other teachers, that I know, meandering through the coaches – teachers heading for the south-west coast to take up their teaching duties .

Every turn of the train displays a scene of beauty as we speed along the beautiful Codroy Valley, between the mountains, beside the open sea, and eventually Port Aux Basques.

As the coastal steamer, the *Bar Haven*, zig-zags its course along the south-west coast, we spend a lot of time viewing the lovely and delightful communities of Rose Blanche, Grand Bruit, Lapoile and other spectacular images. The scenes and human exchanges, as the boat docks, are not unlike that of the Tickle, with one difference- the numbers on the wharf in the Tickle always seem to outnumber any other place. "How ya getting on?"; " Did you have a nice trip?" " How's the fish?" seem to be the order of the day.

We are greeted by the chairman of the board, Mr Phil Matthews, as we disembark at Burgeo. He ushers us to Arch and Susie Collier's where we are catered to and treated kindly for two days and nights while we wait for the Rectory to be prepared. Yes, that's right. I'm not the parson but the Anglican Minister, Rev. Charles Green, has invited us to live with him in the rectory, a beautiful two-storey structure, set back in the garden, a gun–shot from the school.

Rev. Charles is at home when we move in, giving us a brief in-service of the where-with-all of living conditions. He is excited – 'Now I don't have to cook for at least a year,' says he. The hand pump in the kitchen, is demonstrated, the lamps are in their proper brackets and the privy is clean and welcoming.

"My goodness,   . Charles, "It will be some good to have someone to talk t   .ne one to eat with, and someone with whom to share a laugh."

We settle in for our first staff meeting with eleven teachers – Mr. Aubrey Matthews, Vice- Principal, and the mainstay of the school, grew up in Burgeo. He's the one who knows every family, every inhabitant and their background. Mr. Lewis Payne is our utility teacher, a great and thorough educator hailing from Ramea. All the teachers (except myself) hail from the south and south-west coast. They are eager to get started and meet their classes.

I look over some of the names in the registers and I see Benoit, Collier, Dollimount, Cossar, Matthews, Foote, Hann, and on they go.

Every school has to have rules and regulations and this all-grade school at Burgeo is no exception. We add a few new rules as the weeks pass. The one that stands out is, 'No lipstick to be worn by any female student while attending school.' Now there is one thing to make the rule and another to enforce it.

As Principal I'm extremely pleased that things are going so well until this morning in November. I'm in the little office off the senior room when a tap is heard on the door. I open it and Mr. Matthews is standing there and exclaims, "Parsons, it's getting redder and redder."

"What is, Mr. Matthews?"

"The lipstick. What should I do?"

"What do you think?"

"Strap her tomorrow morning if it's worse"

The next morning I hear the commotion in the corridor, and Mr. Matthews appears at the senior room door, where I'm teaching. "Sir, I went to strap her and she took off."

And so began the first test of the lipstick rule. The result was a week of upheaval and finally a peaceful agreement with parents and the student affected. She returned to class and the lipstick rule stuck for the rest of the year.

As time passes we learn about the different areas of Burgeo – the Reach, Muddy Hole, Messers, and the beautiful Sandbanks. Each of these areas has its own identification and uniqueness.

Occasionally Aubrey, his brother, Allan, a storekeeper, and I get one of the local fisherman to take us to White Bear Bay, a spectacle of beauty in its own right. The towering hills, the long inlets, the many ponds literally full of trout make up its characteristics. A day in the bay is therapeutic, refreshing and rejuvenating. And then the boil-up!

Further down the coast is Red Island and Fox Island where the Rev. Charles goes occasionally to hold church service and administer the Holy Communion. In order to do that he has to travel on the steamer.

Yesterday Rev. Charles packed his suitcase, bid us the time of the day and said he would see us in approximately a week. About 11:00 PM he left to board the steamer that was tied up to Burgeo wharf.

This morning Shirley and I are having breakfast when he walks in from his study. "Why, Rev. Charles, what happened?" asks Shirley

"Well, well, well, Mrs. Parsons," he responds, "It was this way. I left and went to the steamer and put my suitcase aboard. The Captain informed me that he was not leaving until 4:00 am; so I came home again, went straight to my study and lay down for an hour or so. Well my dear, it turned out to be a little more than an hour, and when I woke it was 4:10 am; I scravalled as fast as I could over to the boat, but before I got there I could see her going out along by the point; I couldn't believe my eyes. So I ran right to the wharf, walked to the edge and looked down."

Then, even in his disappointment, he burst out laughing, as he always does. He then enjoyed a hearty breakfast.

I'm listening to the *Gerald S. Doyle Bulletin* this evening and I hear a sad story. The announcer reports, "A tragic boating accident today at the little community of Leading Tickles. A fisherman was swept out of his boat by a raging storm and drowned; the other fisherman in the boat managed to get to shore with great difficulty."

A Letter from Home

My Dear Son Cecil,
I don't know how to tell you this but you probably heard it on the radio. Perry Chippett was drowned; the lop just threw him out of the boat in a terrible storm while he and Gordon were on their way in from fishing. You know Gordon Burton, Uncle Garfield's son; that's who was with him. He managed to reach the shore. The whole place is in shock.

Your father is doing good with the fall salmon at Man Point berth but not as good as in May and June.

How is Shirley doing? Look after yourself, and don't go out in the boat. I worry so much about you.

Your loving mother

Wherever we go Shirley always gets herself involved in the community. Besides teaching Sunday school and being a member of the CEWA (the Church of England Women Association), she takes on a whole new challenge.

She has become organizer and leader of the newly formed Girls Auxiliary, this fall of 1958. She, assisted by Delphine Webb, planted the idea of this organization and it has ignited. The group of about thirty-five girls, with their blue skirts, white blouses and GA pin, worn in the center of their ties, have charmed the community not only with their appearances but with their service. Their motto is to develop and foster leadership in church and community.

Girls Auxilary Executive, Burgeo - 1958   *Courtesy of Loretta Green*

Girls Auxilary - Induction Night, Burgeo - 1958 Courtesy of Loretta Green

Actually, hardly a week goes by that Rev. Charles and Shirley don't discuss plans and procedures for improvement in this organization.

There are always people coming from other areas – Gray River, Ramea, etc. to see the 'Parson'. Quite often Shirley has to answer the door, and has information relative to his whereabout. On one occasion, she answered the door and a couple was standing there. The man said, "You must be the parson's new woman. Tell him we wants to get married."

Another day a man from down the coast came to the door; Shirley responded to the knock.

"Is the parson in?" says he. Shirley, not picking up the full expression said, "He's up at the school." He went and came back quickly and said, "Dammit, woman, I'm not looking for Parsons, the teacher, I'm looking for the parson, the minister."

Balancing our time with the school, Church and community, our precious weeks rush by and the Christmas season is just around the corner.

I, as Principal, get an invitation from Mrs. Margaret Lake to attend the fish plant party, in the afternoon on Christmas Eve. I, in turn, invite Mr. Matthews, my Vice-Principal, to go with me since I don't wish to go alone.

Needless to say, it was a lively two hours, with local talent at its best. Besides the usual greetings, story-telling, and folk singing, Mrs Lake asked us if we would like to demonstrate our own individual talents by representing the area from which one hailed. One represented Gaultois, another Francois, and yet another Gray River, and on it continues. This is one time when I wish I had one of the great dancers from the Tickle, like Mike Butler or Arch Rowsell to stand in for me. The fiddler would ask for ones favorite jig, and then "give it to her" as the crowd circled. I represented the Tickle, and Aubrey, Burgeo. Aubrey did a fine job in his representation.

A great afternoon, indeed! I was still home in time to join Shirley and the Rev. Charles at our Christmas Eve supper, and later midnight Mass.

It's now in the dead of the winter, and the parson and I are having one of our many serious discussions. Tonight the talk is about the IWA strike and its impact on the loggers. The radio is on and the announcer says things are getting rough upon the line between the IWA (International Woodworkers of America) and the NBWW (Newfoundland Brotherhood of Woodworkers). It got so bad today that one of the constables from the St. John's Constabulary got struck on the head and is in serious condition.

I have more than a passing interest in this situation since I have two brothers working with the AND Company up on the Bishop's Falls Line. It seems that the International Woodworkers of America is trying to unionize the workers, and Joey, our Premier wants none of it. So he institutes the Newfoundland Brotherhood of Woodworkers.

News From Home

My Dear son Cecil,
I hope you and Shirley are keeping well and looking after yourselves. Your father and I are fine. Your brothers, Wilson and Ronald are home now, thank God. They were both up on the line when all that violence got started between that man, Landon Ladd's crowd and Joey's crowd. I think Wilson attended the IWA meeting and Ronald, the NBWW. My dear, that poor man, Constable Moss, got killed. Imagine what his family is going through. It could have been one of your brothers. What's the world coming to atoll? ....

All my love, Mom

It's June month and school is starting to wind down. It has been a good year both in the school and community.

For the past two days the Christmas Seal has been here doing x-rays and routine medical work. My old friend, Captain Peter Troke, is the Captain on her. Last evening he came to the rectory and stayed for supper; indeed, he stayed until midnight. He remembered the young 'gaffer' in the bed next to him at Twillingate Hospital in 1947 when he was there with his leg smashed up and I was there having my appendix removed. He told me again about his accident on the schooner, and the terrible condition of his leg; all the time he spent in hospital and how Dr. John Olds saved his leg. He also told us many interesting stories that he witnessed around the coast since he became skipper of the Christmas Seal.

We are doing our packing and getting ready to connect with the steamer, go to Port Aux Basques and then back home. Memorial is calling; it's time to refresh and up-grade.

Rev. Charles is sad because we are leaving. So tonight it is time to reminisce and take stock of the past year. And so on it goes, 'Do you remember the night...? Do you remember the time...?'

Yes, Rev. Charles, Shirley and I remember the terrific year we had at Burgeo; we remember having you present with us made it all worth while; we remember you as a kind and gentle spiritual leader as well as a lighthearted human being.

It is a great feeling to be into ones graduating year at Memorial University. Many of us who are in the field of Education and Teacher Training have not completed our years of training consecutively so as to avoid debt build-up. So our pattern has been, for the most part, to do a year of training and then teach for a year or two.

Some of us are now completing our fourth course in Latin and the class is so small we are meeting in Dr. Ashley's office. The students' objective is to prolong the discussion on Caesar's Gallic Wars, *et al*, to avoid having to get into too much translation. We think we are pulling one over on the professor but I'm sure he is fully aware of our strategy.

Shirley has been a great help to me in my Latin translation at home. There are nights, after we climb into bed, she takes the English translation and guides me along while I ponder the Latin. When exhaustion and especially boredom set in, I turn to her and say, *"Gratias, puheler mulier, auxilio tibi as."*

She replies, *"Mea Voluptas, Te amo, Cecilius."*

We both disappear under the bedclothes, oblivious to whether Hannibal and his elephants make it safely across the Alps, or what happened to Caesar on his way to Africa .

The interest in Indian History has stepped up a notch this semester. Dr. Rothany has just returned from that country, where he spent the past year studying their way of life, composition of government and religion. His first hand knowledge of their culture has made for most interesting informational sessions throughout the year.

In one's fourth year of education, and especially teacher training, one is expected to register for and actively participate in the course, 'Philosophy of Education.' Our class is graced with the presence of the Dean, Dr. Hickman, and Dr. Everdon, two well-educated and approachable professors. Needless to say there is little lecturing done and a great deal of discussion taking place.

Most of the students in the class are former teachers and educators who have already gone through smooth sailing and rough seas, and who have definite opinions on what life is all about. We are continuing to seek the truth within these walls. Horace might put it this way, *"Atque inter silvas Academi quaerere verum."* Therefore when such topics as, 'what is our philosophy of education?' or 'what is our philosophy of life?' or 'what is the purpose of life?' are posed, it makes for a lively discussion in a class of thirty or so mature people- people who are ready to go back to the schools and continue instilling prime knowledge into young minds, entrusted to their care. An awesome responsibility !

It is May, 1961 and we, the graduates of Memorial University, approximately one hundred and sixty of us, have assembled in the gymnasium getting ready to parade to St. Patrick's Hall for Convocation. It is a happy and exciting moment in our University lives but it is also a time of saying good-bye, not just to friends but also to the old and cramped University Campus that has served us so well and has done so many students proud. This is the last convocation from her walls. We are told that in September the student body will be moving to the new campus. The students in their dedication to the Old University place a quote by Seumas Vail.

> *There is a golden flow of sunlight in these halls,*
> *An Attic flood of dancing specks of dust,*
> *That fell among the ancient groves of Greece,*
> *Light that was timeless on the dusty roads*
> *Where Plato walked and Horace sought for truth.*
> *That same light fell in Paris long ago*
> *Upon the schools, and shone in Oxford's halls;*
> *And Albert felt that sun and Abelard*
> *And other men too numerous to tell.*
> *Now the light falls upon us where we stand*
> *Among the yellowed books that have been felt*
> *By hands, by minds much greater than our own.*
> *Through them the light transmitted passes down*
> *The dusty corridor of countless years,*
> *The light that always spoke when great men spoke*
> *Among the golden groves of the Academe.*
>   *— Seumas Vail*

Mr Doug Eaton is not only busy trying to line us up but he's also the dispatcher of telegrams of good wishes coming in from the outports around the coasts. When he handed me my seventh telegram he turned and exclaimed, "Who is this Cec Parsons, anyway?" And I am beginning to ask myself the same question. The message from my mom and dad reads, 'Your graduation brings us much honor and praise. Proud to know you did so well. May the Lord bless and guide you in future undertakings. Love and best wishes.'

It seems that the Dean's Office contacts the post office, in this case, in Leading Tickles, to notify the folks of a graduation taking place – maybe the first for a particular place. And the telegrams keep coming – all twenty-three of them.

After the official convocation, Shirley and I are standing around in the annex of the campus on Parade Street, and the Dean walks up to us and he says, "Cecil, have you heard from the Foxtrap school board about a placement for September?"

I say, "No, Dean."

"Give Mr. Clifton Hatcher, the Principal, a call," says he.

When I enquire of Mr. Hatcher he advises me to come see him on Monday night at the Queen Elizabeth Regional High in Foxtrap. After some five minutes of conversation outside the door where the school board meeting is taking place, Mr. Hatcher looks at me and he says, "Parsons, be here in September."

A Letter From Home

My Dear Son Cecil,

I want to congratulate you again on your graduation at the university. You must have gotten a lot of messages from the Tickle; seems like everyone I spoke to, sent you one. Dad and I are doing well. Your father is busy with his salmon nets and getting some fish as well. No trouble to get fish from the cod traps this summer; all you can see are trap-skiffs going up and down through the Tickle, loaded down. Roland and Cecil's skiff, and Uncle Ben's just went by, flat on the water. I think Roland got one of his traps at Bear Cove Head, and Uncle Ben got one at Burnt Island Point.
Are you out on the river again this summer? It must be beautiful there.

Love, Mom

This is my third summer working with the Federal Fisheries Research Board, two of which I have been stationed at North Harbour River in St. Mary's Bay.

The Federal Research cabin is located at a point in the river where the bridge crosses from one side of the community to the other, and where the river deposits its fish and sundry into the harbour and, later, takes on a load returning from the sea.

Let me paint you a scene of picturesque beauty. At five in the morning I walk on the bridge to observe the spectacular modes of sea trout lying in solitude, others jumping in joyful moods, ebbing and tiding making their way along.

I leave for my fifteen-minute walk up the river to a location where the elevator has been installed to trap all the fish that go up and down the river. Our count last year ran into the thousands, and I'm sure it will be the same this year. One can imagine the beauty of the scene – regular sea trout weighing from a pound to three pounds. We hoist the elevator and release them gently.

I am ahead of my story.

I am here as a technician, under the watchful eyes of scientists at the biological station, to help carry out research on the planting, hatching and survival of pink salmon fry in our Newfoundland climatic environment. The biological station plants the eggs in the river in the fall and tracks the journey of the fry, and eventually the salmon, with hopeful returns.

The river for the past two summers has been my home, surrounded by the beauty of nature. It is here we have observed spectacular moments of solitude – a beaver makes its way along the river, a moose grazes on the river bank, a pair of rabbits peer out from behind the bushes, birds sing their songs of love, and trout breech or splash in playful splendor. Nature forces one to be at peace with its environment.

The visitors are many. Some come equipped with expensive rods and reels and get little, while others fish with cheap bamboos and have great success. We were blessed a few days ago with the visit of Dr. Raymond Gushue, President of Memorial University, and some of his friends. I had the pleasure of welcoming him into our cabin for a cup of tea. He was impressed, to say the least, with the research station's experimentation on pink salmon.

Fred Day, the head technician, and I have had some glorious moments on this river as well as on Peter's River, where we have done some ground work for the station.

CHAPTER 6

Queen Elizabeth High Years

As we parade into the gymnasium for our first assembly, I feel honored to be one of the sixteen members of the staff taking our places, each teacher cloaked in a long black gown. Each student is dressed in the appropriate uniform.

Mr. Hatcher opens the assembly and calls upon the Rev. Mark Genge, Chairman of the Board, to do the prayers. He acknowledges each member of the staff, welcomes the students from their respective areas, especially the grade nines who have come together for the first time. He points out to them that this building, the first Regional High School in the Province, will be their home for the next three years.

Some of the students, already there for two years, smile and acknowledge a warm welcome.

Queen Elizabeth Regional High School - 1961

As I look through my roster I see the Pettens, Fagans, Morgans, Dawes, Rideouts, Butlers, Tilleys, Jeffords, to name a few.

The teaching of grade IX geography seems to be my main responsibility for this year – all five classes of it, approximately thirty smiling faces in each class.

My grade IXA class includes such names as John Richards, Grace Dawe, Sam Mercer, Ken Cole, Connie Barnes. Today after class, I give back their tests that they did two days ago. At the end of the class Kenny comes up to me, and in his unassuming manner, says in a soft voice, "I think you have this 'complete the blank' statement marked right and my answer is wrong."

I say, "You are right, Kenny, and that will now leave you with a total mark of 98% instead of 100%."

It's certainly a pleasant task to teach those students who take the hall of learning seriously. Not only are they serious in their approach but they demonstrate the highest respect for their teachers. I have learned a long time ago that good relationships between the teacher and students can only be attained if respect is shown all around.

We received the shock of our lives today. One of our colleagues, Mr. Herbert Haines, died suddenly, while teaching his students. He was doing something he always loved to do – imparting knowledge to the youth. The students in their dedication wrote, "We pay tribute to a great man who won the love and respect of us all."

I have the responsibility of instructing a Grade X class in the knowledge of Church History. This particular morning my voice is not so good and one of my students, Olga, offers to do the class for me. She not only does a fine job on the lesson but she mimics her teacher, skillfully, wetting her fingers and fixing loose strands of hair that her teacher usually has, falling out of place. As well, she does the stance and other idiosyncrasies the teacher is known for.

"If you don't mind, class," she says, "I'll read from the text to see if we can get the drift as to why Henry the VIII managed to end up with so many wives..." A pleasant and wholesome presentation, indeed! And we all enjoyed the change.

I stand in awe, sometimes, as I walk through the corridors of this great Queen Elizabeth Regional High School and see the many facilities awaiting our students. They are so blessed to have access to so many sports and co-curricular activities – basketball, volleyball, badminton, and regular gym activities in the timetable. As well, down in the basement are the bowling alleys. Then there are the gym prefects, the library prefects, the yearbook committee and the Queen Elizabeth Army Cadets.

Queen Elizabeth Regional High School Staff - 1963

Added to all of the above, is an outstanding body of students that one can't help loving. The majority are courteous, show great respect for their teachers, and get along fine with each other.

In order for any high school, Queen Elizabeth High, not withstanding, to be able to inherit such a fine body of students, teachers in the various small feeder schools from Paradise to Seal Cove must have done a fine job of teaching and imparting knowledge and training.

I am looking at one of the year books now and the salutation reads, "The elementary schools constitute the most important part of our school program. We are very anxious that a good foundation is built... This can only be made a reality when all parents and teachers work together as partners in one great school system."

I have already met some of these great teachers and educators: Mr. Jack Richards, Principal of St. Albans school in Kelligrews – longtime community leader; Mr, Ray Mercer, Vice-Principal of St. Albans School, a community leader, and a great story teller; Mr. Jessie Blackmore, Principal of the local school in Chamberlains – lay-reader and community leader; Mr. Frank French, Principal of St. Georges School in Long Pond; Mr .Linos Green, Mr. Ken Smith, Mrs. Margaret Rowe, Ms. Alice Payne, to name a few. They are indeed serving their communities and schools well.

This morning I'm sitting here in the upper staff room preparing a lesson during my period off from the classroom. I'm feeling a bit tired because I had a rough night. A few days ago Shirley and I brought our infant daughter home for the first time. Oh yes, after eight years without child, there are now three of us in the family.

Around three o'clock this morning daughter, Debra decides she wants company. So I try not to disturb Shirley, who usually gets up; I creep out, fetch our darling from her crib, only to realize she needs changing. So I get rid of the dirty one and try to install another. What a major undertaking! First I spread it out full length, then I try to fold but corners are not coming out right. In the meantime the mite is cooing and lying there as if daring me to do the wrong thing.

I finally roll our special gift in her fancy blanket and take her in my arms, rocking away, wondering what the future will hold for her, and how her presence will make changes in our lives.

Like I say, I'm preparing a lesson in the upper room, I'm alone and I glance across to the far corner of the room, towards Mr. Frank George's desk and I see his briefcase sitting there, but just a moment, it's moving on its own. I shake my head, and now I know I had a rough night. I keep writing but my eyes keep wondering in the same direction, and again the case is dancing. I think to myself, 'I'm not that far gone.' So I jump up and move toward the corner just in time to witness the head of a kitten appearing from out of the briefcase. I smile to myself, and I know that Mr. Best has been up to his tricks again.

Mr. Evans, in the '65 Pioneer yearbook, writes, "If all efforts end with graduation, we might well ask... what's the use? As students, we are leaving high school to enter a competitive world, ... our motto must be *"carpe diem"* – to seize every chance, whether big or small, to prepare ourselves for the role we must play in the work-a day-world."

To further his thoughts, later, Mr. Evans emphasizes the need for more efficient streaming of students but this, he points out, "will

Homeroom class 1965 - Note uniforms and black gown worn by the homeroom teacher.

depend upon trained personnel in the form of guidance counselors and small classroom units".

Our graduates go on to new challenges that seem to become more varied each passing year. Many of our students go on to Memorial University, where they enroll in varying disciplines and degree programs. Many go to technology and vocational institutes, and still others go directly into the workforce.

Whatever direction these approximately one hundred graduates take, the school is now becoming aware of the need for more formal help in the school setting. Mr. Evans, the Principal, approaches me, and asked me if I would become more familiar with admission requirements to Post Secondary Institutions, and gather more literature for the library on the world of work. Under the direction of the Principal, and co-ordinated by a staff committee a career night is organized, at least once a year, at which time personnel from the University come and make themselves available to the senior students, who come along at night and ask questions relative to their interests about the world of work after high school.

It's not all work for the students at Queen Elizabeth. Quite often they are involved in extracurricular activities that lend laughter and relaxation, not only for the students but also for the teachers as well.

TWIRP Week is one of those times when students plan a whole lot of fun activities – competition in volleyball and other sports between students and students, as well as between students and teachers. In the case of the volleyball the 'Tin-can Trophy' is at stake, and the teachers hate to lose in the play-offs. Again there is the 'Lollipop Trophy' in bowling – a hard-fought game and a well sought-after prize.

It's a time when teachers as well as students go on public display and act 'fools' in an entertaining way. Skits and candid shots become the order of the day. At the closing of a week of TWIRP activities the crowning of the TWIRP Week King and Queen have become ever so popular. And you ask any young man what TWIRP stands for, and he says with great emphasis 'The Woman Is Requested to Pay.'

During the dance practically all the teachers, with their spouses, attend. It is a fun-filled night, with teachers trying to do the latest in the dancing arena. It is not unusual seeing students teaching teachers how to do the twist or the jive. Then again we sometimes have a brave soul among the female students who attempt a step-dance with one of the more aging male teachers. Pretty well any thing is tried when it comes to 'scuffing,' and it's amazing how much it lends to improved pupil-teacher relationships in the class-room, and in the school generally.

A Letter From Home

My Dear Son Cecil,

How are you, Shirley and Debbie? She must be cute; kiss the dear for me. Ron and Tootsie have four children now, and Wilson and Myrtle have three. There seems to be a lot in the 'family way' those days.

Dad is getting his hauling rope ready; I think there's a few seals on the ice. My dear, the ice is raftered so much you can walk to Cape John.

Cecil, I have to tell you that Uncle Fred Rowsell passed away. You know the man who owned the Union Store.

Say hello to Charlotte for me. I guess she's graduating in June.

Love, Mom

I think about Uncle Fred who used to hire us, even when he didn't have much work for us to do. But we would ask him and he could-n't say no. What a good man.

Charlotte, Shirley's sister who has been staying with us for the past three years, attending Queen Elizabeth Regional High School, is completing her grade eleven and is planning to go to Leamington, Ontario for work. It seems we have quite a number of Newfoundlanders these years heading for Central Canada. We will miss her because she has been a very important part of our family.

Charlotte Clarke
QE Graduate - 1965

We are down in the Tickle this summer for a holiday, and I take advantage of every opportunity to go on the water. Wilson and Will are fishing together, doing deep water trawl. So while the trawl is being hauled and the cod fish keep shining and floating upon the water, Wilson and Will take turns spinning yarns, especially about their fishing and sealing experiences. I know there are times when they are trying to put one over on me.

Wilson says, "Cecil, this is a true story but it don't make much sense, it's more like a riddle. This is the way it was told to me by our friend Robert."

> *Pulled up off of Double Island*
> *Took out a big bun and commenced the gnaw*
> *Twasn't long for up he shoves*
> *Sling she goes*
> *And out he kegs*
> *Pull Pop pull*

I say, "Wilson, you better unravel that; I'm lost."

Wilson says, "Cecil, my boy, it's this way, according to what we can discern from Robert:

"Father and me went out swiling (sealing); we rowed that old punt up toward Seal Bay until we got off Double Island. Then we got a bit leary (hungry), so we opened the bread-box and took out a fat pork bun and commenced (started) to gnaw (eat). It wasn't long before a seal pokes his head above water and father gaffles (grabs) the old gun, pulls the cock (of the gun) out of the dog (notch) and fires. The load strikes the swile (seal) and flattens it like a keg on the water. I said father, pull as hard as you can before that seal sinks."

I say, "Wilson I understand now, but what do you mean by the cock and the dog of the gun?"
"Will boy, the cock is the hammer; most people in the Tickle call it the cock. You pull it back half way and there's a safety catch where you can set the hammer and she won't fire. The safety catch we call the dog notch. When you're in a hurry to shoot you only got half the distance to pull the cock."

"That sounds sensible, Wilson; now it's your turn, Will." I think Will is about to tell about the two guys who started building a house at daylight and by dark had the job finished, and was carrying the stove up over the hill to have it installed. But just a moment. A couple of whales are blowing around the boat. Wilson and Will are not paying much attention to them but I am. So the conversation turns to the mammals and what they are up to now.

The year 1966 has been designated as 'Come Home Year' by our Provincial Government, and our students at Queen Elizabeth High School have not been found wanting in their appeal to the ex-

Newfoundlanders to return to their birthright. Here is a poem that I have chosen and published with permission.

Welcome Home
by Betty Tibbo , Grade IX

Ye Newfoundlanders far and near,
We want you all to know,
This is the year we're going all out
To put on a great big show.

We have the supper all prepared
Scruncheons, with fish 'n' brews,
I'll tell you boys it will compare
With "the spree at Kelligrews".

Caplin, lobsters, toutens too,
A 'boil up' on the beach
Anything that your 'hearts desire'
Will be within your reach.

Joey will give his finest speech
We'll dance the lancers too;
We'll raise the roof with 'I'se the Bye'.
And we'll open up the 'Brew'.

The boys from Petty Harbour
Wilf Doyle and all his band
Will warm the 'cockles of your heart'
With the music of our land.

Scammell will sing "The Squid Jiggin' Ground"
Dr. Story will propose the toast
Uncle Mose will tell you a story or two
Me 'n Ned will get ready 'The Roast'.

So come on back to your native isle
To the people you love so dear
And let's make this a 'whale of a time'
In this our 'Come Home Year'.

To add to the invitation Paul Dean, a grade XI student, reports on the state of the fishery in the waters of Newfoundland.

Old Joe Antle got a quintal
Johnny Crew got a few
Billy J'arn, he got n'arn
And that was all was caught this marn'

A Letter From Home

My Dear Son Cecil,

How are you, Shirley and Debbie? I bet Debbie is a big girl now and the treasure of your hearts. Your father and I are looking forward to you coming in November when you get the long week-end. Your father says there is a good sign of puffins and the odd turr. By the time you get here they'll be thick enough.

Your father got a two-headed boat now; she looks some queer.

Love, Mom

I have to be honest about my feelings; I can hardly wait to get down to the Tickle and go out after the turrs. I can always count on my mother not to let me forget my roots. God bless her; she's a darling.

It is now Remembrance Holiday weekend and we arrived here yesterday, with snow flurries all the way along.

Let me tell you we have had quite a day of it. Father wasn't so well today so Ches Forsey volunteered to go out birding with me in father's two-headed boat with a four Acadia engine in her. It was rough enough out around Legge Rock today in a one-headed one but in this one it was like one was sitting on the lop all the time.

I've been out on the water when it's been pretty rough after turrs but today 'cut the cake'. In case you don't know, after a 'north-easter blow' like we just had, a swell and lop form in the water and today when the boat used to go down in the trough (hole) one couldn't see land or other boats near by. Ches was in his glee.

Uncle Herbert Rowsell at Leading Tickles, selling poppies - 1966

That wasn't so bad but the engine wasn't working properly. Every now and then it would shut off. Ches had to get the copper tube off and blow and suck until the gas got through again.

Mother has got the pan on now frying the hearts and livers of the forty-odd turrs.

Father says, "Cecil, I know your eyes wasn't out on your cheeks with all that swell, the rolling of the boat, and the engine shutting off and all." I just smile because I know he is right. Uncle Stu and Aunt Win are here having a cup of tea, and he's 'minding' the time when he and father used to run the fish and passenger boat to Point Leamington. I remember, as well, the good time I used to have going with them, as a child.

Uncle Herb Roswell, that's Aunt Violet's Uncle Herb, just came in to say hello. He's making the rounds selling poppies.

Uncle Herb is a veteran of the first World War, and every year he sells the poppies. He also visits the sick and shut-ins. Here is a man who shows a lot of concern for the well-being of the total community, and his visits inspire many through his caring and gentle encouragement.

CHAPTER 7

Changes and Progress

This summer of 1967 I find myself representing the school as a teacher sponsor for Allied Youth at Berwick, Nova Scotia. So Shirley, daughter, Debra, and I, with student representatives, Alvin Chubb and Joyce Dawe, are in camp with dozens of others in the Atlantic Region, learning about this worthwhile activity.

We have quite a number of students at Queen Elizabeth High interested in this activity which had its origin back in August, 1964. It all started when Linda Dawe and Glenn Taylor attended an Allied Youth camp. They learned that its objective was to "seek the truth concerning beverage alcohol and the best way of life in relation to this problem." They also learned that one can have a lot of fun without drinking. They were sold on the idea. And so was Mr. Frank George and Ms. Gertrude Sellers, the first teacher sponsors for the first post of students at Queen Elizabeth High. They attended the International Conference in Washington, D.C. The school had the honor of being host to the second Provincial Conference of Allied Youth, 1965.

Like I said before, we are having a great time in camp and enjoying the fellowship, and learning experiences. The idea is not to preach to our students about the abuse of alcohol but rather to let them know, through the literature and seminars, what adverse effects alcohol can do to our bodies in relationship to our well-being.

It's back to school time and we are up in the "Upper Room', our staff room, exchanging stories of what had transpired over the summer. Heber Best brought up about our fishing trip during the summer, and Frank George suggested we should not tell it but recite his poem he had composed. Back in July I encouraged Heber, Frank and his son, Carl to go with me to North Harbour River in St. Mary's Bay to angle the big sea trout. After spinning the yarn about my wonderful experiences with the Fisheries Research and my involvement with the big trout, they were convinced. We did spend a night with our tent pitched on the river bed. The result of that visit is Mr. Frank George's poem.

DAWN, SUNDAY, 16 July, 1967

> Early one morning before the sun was shining
> I crept from the tent and tried to catch some trout,
> While Cecil and Heber were snoring in their blankets
> And dreaming of the big ones they catch when they got out.
>
> Chorus: Oh! Do not wake me. Never forsake me.
>   Why do you treat a sleepy fellow so.
>
> Heber's dreams were shattered by noises from the river.
> Alarmed, he woke Cecil in hushed and whispered tones,
> "I fear we're in danger - where did you put that hatchet?
> There's something big or someone out walking
>   on the stones.

The terrified pair listen awhile...

> Says he I'm sure a poacher has his net across the river.
> It must be several dozen I've heard him heave ashore.

Ah! Now he comes nearer. Where is your coleman cooker?
Oh! Heber, — (It's brand new) —outside the tent door.

Send Frank out to get it. We're better without him.
If he's killed by the poacher, we'll have no regrets.
Well! Damn, if he's not missing.
        Old "Jam Mouth" has deceived us.
He's caught all our trout. Oh! I'll kill that bugger yet."

They rushed from the tent, grabbed their rods
        in the darkness;
But try as they might, not a rise could they get.
The sea trout weren't running. They tried for some
        mud trout
But the loot from their trip, they would rather forget.

A great piece of poetry, indeed, and certainly as it happened. Mr George is older than most of the teachers in the school but he is younger at heart than many. His teaching experiences have been most interesting, and quite often he will relate stories about his early years in teaching. I think I've been privileged because he allows me to peek into his diary that he has kept faithfully over the years. Here is one of his episodes as he relates it during his teaching year in Lamaline.

Lamaline 1932-33

Lamaline East (Muddy Hole) had a one-room all-grade school. The east side school was a drafty old building with a minimum of equipment and resources. It was heated by a pot-bellied stove situated in the middle of the room.

On the afternoon of my arrival at Lamaline I deposited my meager belongings at my prearranged boarding house, inquired about the school board representative for Lamaline East and then went to see him. He, a store manager, was busy in his office so I was given some time to cool my heels and get acquainted with the lady clerks after one of them announced my presence. When admitted to the office we both mutually introduced ourselves and shook hands. I was astounded by his first remark. "So you're the new teacher. Are you any good to fight?" After an awkward pause I replied, "I'm not fond of fighting but if I get into one I try my damnest not to come out second best."

"That's the spirit," he said "You'll do." Thus I made my first good friend in Lamaline and he continued to give me information about the place and its people. He inquired about my habits, whether I smoked or drank and warned me about getting mixed up in the brawls and fights which were commonplace there because alcohol was so easy to get. Right there and then I asked him the price of rum and cigarettes in St. Pierre. From his answers I said I would like for him to get me two bottles of 75 cent rum and two cartons of $1.75 cigarettes by the first party he knew of that was going to St. Pierre. He knew that Bill, the operator of a store along the road a bit farther, was sending a party out sometime soon and he would like to place an order with Bill for himself. He wrote a note of intro-duction and sent me along to Bill with it. Everything worked out fine. I was to get my baccy and rum much cheaper than from a bootlegger.

A few days later Bill sent a note by one of my pupils to pick up a parcel at the store after school. I guess I broke the all-time walking record hurrying to that store. In the office we put the rum in a large gaiter box, opened the cartons of cigarettes and stowed as many packs as we could in with the rum and I pocketed the remainder. After a pleasant drink, a smoke and a chat, I left for home. Lo and behold, about half way home here was the uniformed arm of the law bearing down on me. Hugging my box close to my chest I said "Good evening constable," and tried to hurry on. "What are you carrying in that box?" he asked. I never came as close to a heart attack again as I did at that moment. "You can see by the carton that I have a new pair of gaiters." "A likely yarn," he said. "Buying gaiters in early September. You expecting an early winter?" "In case it is I like to be prepared for it way ahead of time," I replied. "No doubt you do but I think I will go along with you to see if your new gaiters fit." Silently I prayed that the earth would open up and swallow one of us up, preferably him. There was no way out of it. I was caught red-handed. I was doomed to be jailed as a smuggler since I had no money to pay a fine. I had invested all my spare money in rum and cigarettes. He fell in beside me and we marched to my boarding house.

I introduced him to the family, went to my bedroom, picked up a pack of legal cigarettes, returned to the kitchen and offered him one. He accepted. We lit up and I strained every nerve trying to keep up a conversation to distract him from the carton. Soon, however, he said, "Now it's time for me to see those gaiters. Open up," I asked the mistress if we could go into the parlor as I did not want the family to witness my transgression. She consented, after making excuses about it not being fit to receive visitors. We entered the sanctum and hesitantly I exposed the loot. "Now," he said, "I'll have to sample this liquor." He expertly popped the cork out of one bottle. "You go and get a jar of water and two glasses." I obeyed his order and before long one of my precious rum bottles was empty and we were quite tipsy and 'feeling no pain.'

He helped himself to three packs of cigarettes which he said he also had to sample, wished me good luck and departed. I breathed a sigh of relief for having escaped arrest.

Next evening I visited Bill's store again and after telling him all about my brush with the law he had a hearty laugh at it and informed me it was all a 'put up' job. The two storekeepers had set me up to be waylaid by the policeman just to give me a helluva fright and see how I would react to it. "Boy," I said, "It's a wonder you didn't scare me to death. As it is I think you took ten years off my life."

"Sorry old chap about that but here is another bottle of rum to replace the one you lost. The trick was well worth it."

"How come you could get the constable to cooperate with you sleveens when he knew it was smuggled goods you were peddling to me?" I asked.

"You see," Bill said, "the police are only after the big bootleggers, not the insignificant, little smugglers like you and I. If the authorities could catch every petty smuggler, 90% of the men on this coast would be jailbirds; so they have to ignore the small stuff unless somebody lays a complaint." I was known to the trio as Rummy after that episode

Each year at Queen Elizabeth High brings with it changes to our school system. New teachers come and other teachers move out, seeking greener pastures. Graduates disperse and go their separate ways, grade IXs move in to fill the spaces vacated by the new present tens.

One notable thing is that the numbers are increasing and our school is bursting at the seams.

Our curriculum has become more diversified. The number of students doing French has sky-rocketed. Our centennial year may have had some influence on the increased interest, with so much publicity on two official languages and the need for bi-lingualism in the federal domain.

Fashions are creeping into the classrooms. The mini-skirt is beginning to reveal itself more, and in some cases getting shorter and shorter. Two grade IX students, Mary Fagan and Carol Walsh tell it nicely in their poem:

The Dizzy World of Fashions

The mini skirts are all the style
They look so very neat
But they are not convenient
When on a busy street.

The skirts they are so very tight
Getting in them is a squeeze,
They didn't have much material
Being far above the knees.

With mini-skirts you watch your step,
You can't do as you please
You always have to hold your breath
You can't afford to sneeze.

Short skirts are going out
The hems are down a bit,
Button boots are coming back
The girls will throw a fit.

The eyes are well protected
This fashion never fades
Each year there's something new
Such as the Monkee shades.

Styles are like stock markets
Going up and down
From a micro-mini skirt,
To a granny gown.

Mr. Tom Pope has taken over as Principal of Queen Elizabeth High, and he brings with him a wealth of information and new ideas. The school programing is diversifying more and more; the vocational section in the library is expanding, and more of the literature on the world of work is readily available. Students are no longer satisfied with what teachers tell them about the world of work and about the need for certain courses. They want to find out for themselves by asking more questions, and reading up more on the new material.

Memorial University is no longer just for someone else; the students are beginning to set their sights and establish goals. Career nights are becoming recognized as an important aspect of finding out 'what's going on'. The students gather around in groups to listen to professors speak about careers, or they approach the personnel and ask questions. On one such occasion we see a professor in a discussion with Stan, one of our students. Later the professor approaches two or three of us gathered around and inquires, "Parsons, that student to whom I was just talking, he must be at the University level doing Chemistry? He is so well informed."

"No, professor, he's doing Grade XI general science; but that's the kind of students we produce here." We all get a hearty chuckle out of it.

I am happy to say that I've been appointed to the Atlantic Marking Board this summer of 1968. The marking is taking place at Acadia University in Wolfville, Nova Scotia. It is here that all the grade XI Public Examinations are marked, coming in from the four Atlantic Provinces – Newfoundland, Prince Edward Island, New Brunswick and Nova Scotia. I, with a number of other teachers, have been assigned to the marking of Latin. It is not just a marking experience but a learning environment. We not only mark the papers but we discuss the various approaches to the teaching of this classical language. An added bonus is that we get to sit and talk with some of the best scholars in the field of teaching.

I might add that we have a Provincial Marking Board back in St. John's, Newfoundland for the purpose of marking grades IX and X Examinations. A Center is selected in the city and dozens of teachers are assigned from all over the Province to come together for assessing and grading. I was privileged to have had two summers previously assigned to the Provincial Board.

In his second year as Principal, Mr. Tom Pope calls me in his office and suggests that I should get serious about guidance and maybe seek special training. I do take his advice seriously, and apply to be admitted to the University of New Brunswick in their program of Guidance and Counseling .

Our daughter Debra's Kindergarten Graduation - 1969 St. George's School

It is late September, 1969 and we are happy to report that our daughter, Debra, graduated back in June; yes, graduated from her kindergarten program, and she has the certificate to prove it. Things, however, didn't quite go right on her first day in grade one in this school year. She came home from her first day and emphatically announced to her mother and me that she would not be returning to school any more. We suggested to her that such a move would leave her a grade one drop-out, and it didn't seem the proper thing to do. After some back and forth exchange, she consented to returning. "I'll finish this year to please you and dad," she pronounced.

"Thank goodness," says her mother, "we'll deal with next year when it comes."

Anyway, Debra just came through the door dressed in her Brownie uniform, and she is a charmer. I have to listen, with great interest, what they did in Brownies this evening. I've heard it before but there are bound to be new developments, and an activity in Brownies that really excited her this evening.

Debra, giving the salute

Shirley, as well, is coming through the door in her Guider's uniform. Back in 1964 she took on the role of Snowy Owl, and the next year Brown Owl. Now she is District Commissioner for Kelligrews and Upper Gullies. According to the smile on her face, she is enjoying it.

I turn to opening my mail, and there is a letter from my mother. Like I said before, I get a letter from her at least every three weeks and she keeps me informed of family affairs, as well as community developments. She tells me about sick people, anyone that has passed away, how they are doing with the fish, seals, lobsters, who is in the 'family way', etc.

For the past two or three years she has been keeping me up to date on the highway being built from Point Leamington to Leading Tickles. In 1966, she wrote, *"Cecil. You'll soon be able to drive right to the South Side. There are talks that they might just build a causeway across the Ladle; then you'll be able to drive on the island. Oh my, we are really getting modern."*

Later she writes, *"Cecil, if we could only get the electricity here so that I can run my fridge and stuff instead of waiting for Jack Ward to turn on the generator. The only time we can see a bit of television is in the night when the engine is on, and then she's off more than she's on."*

And now this letter tonight reads, *"Cecil, my son, we are finally connected. You won't have to leave your car on the South Side and come over in boat. You can drive across on the causeway to the Island and park on Parsons' Hill. Thank God."* Mother has that jovial way with her that makes me want to be near her and wrap my arms around her. A wonderful mom with unconditional love.

It's September, 1970 and the beginning of our second year at the new Queen Elizabeth High on the Foxtrap Access Road. We have just assembled for our first staff meeting and we are doing the usual greetings and salutations. New faces have appeared in the gathering and some familiar faces are absent.

The one familiar face that is not with us this year is Frank George. He retired in June after nine years serving faithfully the school and the students intrusted to his care. When students referred to 'Mr. George' it was with much affection and high respect.

Besides making his mark on Queen Elizabeth High he taught in sixteen other places around the Province such as Happy Adventure, Port De Grave, Trout River, and Norris Point, to name a few. He started teaching in 1926 and celebrated his sixteenth birthday the same year. He also served the communities in other capacities – army cadet leader, church duties including lay reader, onstage drama, *et al,* and more.

The students of Queen Elizabeth in their tribute thank him most sincerely 'for your contributions as a fine educator, a parent and a great humanitarian.'

Like I said we have just gathered, and the Principal, Mr. Albert Chaulk, draws attention to the agenda, and specifically to new programing. He states that one of the roles of the new guidance counselor is to help students fit into the program. One of our teachers, in all innocence, and without being facetious, asks, "And what will the counselor do for the rest of the year after all the students are programed?" He looks at the Principal for an answer, and the Principal looks at me. After all I have been just recently appointed by the board on a full time basis, and the question keeps repeating itself – What is a Counselor? What does he do? Is this person going to make a difference or is it a waste of a classroom unit? I could respond with flowery rhetoric and launch into some theories of the effectiveness of counseling. My response, however, is, "We'll have to wait and see."

Indeed, the very idea of hiring counselors for schools is rather new to the province. Mr. Fred Kirby, recently appointed Superintendent of the Conception Bay South Integrated School System, is innovative and has long range plans for education under his care. Guidance and counseling, with other important services, is on his agenda. Some of the larger schools in St. John's have only recently assigned such personnel.

Last year I was allocated ten periods for vocational guidance, but this year it will include much more. This year personal one on one counseling and group guidance will be the order of the days and weeks ahead.

It's October and I get a call from a mom that she had found a referral note in her son's pocket to see the guidance counselor, but that there was nothing wrong with his head. So why was this necessary.

I try to explain that her son had been referred by the Principal about program change and that his mind was fine. She sounded relieved, somewhat, but there was still some uncertainty. I know I will experience incidents like this until parents become familiar with 'what the counselor is doing.' Frequent phone calls of concerns that keep coming will, I'm sure, diminish in number when parents realize that their son or daughter is being helped in the process. Of course, the most important witness is the student himself

I realize, all too well, that the counselling process will have to be sold and proven to all – teachers, administration, parents, and most of all the students.

Another first for the school is a careers day organized and arranged to take place during school time. It seems to have gone off successfully under the direction of the guidance committee, supported by the administration. Booths were set up in the gymnasium and manned by professional resource people invited to the school. Students are allowed to take time out from the classroom activities to visit, observe the displays and talk with a person about the career of most interest to them.

Students seem to catch on to this approach and use it wisely to help consolidate their thoughts about future career planning.

A Letter From Home

My Dear Son Cecil,

I do hope you are all keeping well. Kiss Debbie for me.

Thank God I can finally plug in my fridge and know that it will stay on. Yes, my dear, the electricity has finally reached the Tickle. What a blessing! Now I can watch my favourite program – Another World, and Don Messer and his Islanders. I can turn the lights on now when I get out of bed at night instead of having to light the lamp. Oh yes, and I can have toast in the toaster.

My dear, I don't know how to tell you this but Chess Forsey passed away, only a young man. Remember how he took you out birding one time. And poor old Dummy Gill he passed away too. How could you possibly forget him, the dear man. Many a time he made you boys afraid signing about ghost stories and stuff. And Aunt Caroline Noseworthy, the dear soul, she passed away too.

My dear, I was telling you about the new school that they are building here, a school for the younger children. They will soon have it ready to open. No doubt they will be sending the senior students to Point Leamington.

*   Love, Mom*

We are now into a vibrant and productive year all around at Queen Elizabeth High. One might call it the add-on year because so many things are happening around us, so much excitement in the air, so many things with which to become involved.

Mr. Reg Tilley is the new Principal, assisted by Mr George Evans, and Ms. Beverly Pope as assistant Vice-Principal. The staff has increased to twenty-six. The school is offering pretty well most things in sports activities. Then we have the Drama Club, a newspaper called the Queens Page, Photography Club, Allied Youth, Sewing Club, Chess Club, Speech and Debating, Reach for the Top, and the list goes on.

Our curriculum has broadened to include Industrial Arts and Home Economics. And on a more specific spectrum we have joined forces with Roncalli Central High in Avondale to send our Grade IX students to the Vocational School in Seal Cove to explore pre-vocational education. Each grade IX student is given the opportunity to chose one course from seven different courses: Woodworking, Metalworking, Cooking, Sewing, Beauty Culture, Typing, Drafting.

Again the lot falls to the guidance counselor to help co-ordinate this program and liaise with the instructors and administration at Seal Cove Vocational School. So the Counselor finds himself sitting in meeting after meeting with administrators, other guidance personnel, skilled and professional people at the Trade School and professionals from the Department of Vocational Education.

Special Education has also become a very important area in our school system. Students having learning disabilities may now find a more satisfying environment in those smaller classes with more specific programming. The school is also blessed to have two highly skilled and trained teachers to teach and relate to those students.

To keep the school environment more pleasing and more exciting, dances are held on a more scheduled basis, concerts and plays are becoming more commonplace. Most teachers offer themselves to help out in extracurricular activities. In addition, teachers and students 'let off steam' at certain times of the year in relaxation activities. For example, during the pre-Christmas 'on the stage get-together', the students gather in the gymnasium to watch the teachers perform the Twelve Days of Christmas as well as other selections. Yes, therapy sessions are happening and it's lending support for better student-teacher relationships.

Teachers have their own therapeutic sessions away from the students when the school day is at an end, and more specifically on Friday afternoon when rituals take place. There is the birthday dunk when the teacher in question, whose birthday it is, goes through a dipping ceremony, and there is no choice in the matter. A large tub of water is provided and the birthday person, more specifically the male species, is taken, 'kicking and flicing' (flousing) and deposited in the tub of water with a simple ceremony. Bumping is optional.

Other shennanigns that the author will not detail are the water-soaked chair, and the installing of the secret hole, the misdirected phone calls. Let me cite an example of the latter. I mentioned to Mr. Best, prior to the Christmas break, that I needed a Christmas tree that was perfectly symmetrical and he advised me to call a specific number. I follow his advice and dialed the number. The person on the other end of the phone answered, "This is the funeral home."

Another prank that continues the rounds is that of the 'phantom student'. A couple of teachers take a blank examination paper belonging to another teacher, without the teacher being aware of it, and completes the 'fill in blanks,' 'multiple choice,' or whatever; they then slip it into the pile. They either have the answers all wrong or all right. They call this an 'alertness activity.'

These 'lark sessions' always made for good psychological therapy, and a belly full of laughs, thus promoting harmony and good-will among the teachers involved.

Queen Elizabeth High, like other schools, I'm sure, seems to reach out and take possession of both teachers and students alike; thus leaving most of them speaking fondly of her, and with deep respect. Jeffrey Hiscock, in his valedictory speech said, "... we will always feel proud when we hear her name mentioned.... Remember Queen Elizabeth is what you make her and she has always been strong."

Judy Petten, as valedictorian of '72 says, "But I know we'll all come back this way some day, for you can never leave something as dear to you as Queen Elizabeth without wanting to return, even just for a visit."

A number of student activities seems to be taking the spotlight these days. The 'Between Ourselves' program, prepared by students and broadcast over the school public address system every Friday, is creating a high interest. This activity is under the direction of the Speech and Debating Club and Mr. Robert Dawe. Students air their views and express their concerns, but do it in a responsible manner.

The School Paper, *"Queens Page,"* dubbed the voice of the student, allows the students freedom of expression.

The Speech and Debating Club has become more directly involved in special activities outside the school as well as within the school. Participation in the Conception Bay South Lions Club Speak-Out takes front center. Eva Hillier, an outstanding leader in the school, is the winner of the first Lions Club Speak-out, hosted by the Lions Club.

An activity, that seems to lighten up the walls of Queen Elizabeth is the entertainment, put forward by the 'Clodd Squad' a group determined to liven up the place and boost the morale of both teachers and students.

They organize their own music and perform skits, etc., to the delight of the student body.

Another activity that seems to have come into its own this school year of 1973-74 is the Drama Club. Talent on stage seems to abound with more and more students not only showing interest but many participating on stage. It's not easy to forget the presentation of the play, 'The Witches' and the super performance of the students.

The activity that got started back in the '60s and has kept rolling along ever since is the Allied Youth, a very worthwhile organization. It has been a program that has meant many things to many students. To some it means getting to understand the wise use of alcohol, to others it means friendship, travel, and still to others it means socializing in a responsible manner. Whatever the reason it has played a positive role for many Pioneers over the years.

The Guidance Department is becoming more involved, expanding and taking on a face of its own. A Peer Guidance Committee, made up of four responsible senior students, is making a worthwhile contribution to the guidance functioning. These caring students dis-

Student Guidance Assistants - 1974

tribute appointments, organize the guidance material and look after it, and do a fine job of enhancing the cause of a helping situation.

Here is Brenda Gullage with her message.

"Hi students. As many of you are aware, the Guidance Department has been, through the year, ready and willing to aid you in your in your problems – vocational, educational and personal. Our Committee consisted of five other teachers as well as four grade eleven students. Many of you have had problems this year and have been helped through the Guidance Department... We have found it a honor and great privilege to help and serve you the student body. May your years ahead be successful and fulfilling, and may you, the Graduates, consider taking 'the road less traveled by.' "

I have to pay tribute to another group of resource people that I consider to be part of the expanded Guidance and Helping Team. The

Public Health Nurses – Elizabeth Avery and Enid Barrett – are professionals in their field. Not only do they visit Queen Elizabeth on a regular schedule but they come whenever they are needed.

The same may be said for the Social Workers who enhance the guidance role by seeing and counseling students that come under their care, and students that are referred by the Guidance Department and Administration of the school.

Sometimes we have to bring the total helping services into play to help the student that has gone astray.

Our daughter, Debra and I are into conversation about St. Georges School and her teachers. She is telling me how much she enjoys Mr. French's humour when he comes to their class, and she attempts to tell some of the jokes.

It's around 8:00 P.M. and the phone rings, I reach to answer it, and the voice on the other end says, "Hello my dear."

"Is that you, mom? Where are you calling from? Are you down at the Railway Station in St John's? Why didn't you tell me you were coming on the train?"

She laughs that hearty laugh, "Why, Cecil, I'm calling you from home on my own phone. We had the phones connected today, thank God. I can now call you instead of having to write you. It seems like every time I call you I got bad news. Dummy Fred passed away, my dear; the poor man, he worked so hard in his day. I think I told you a while back about Uncle Fred Guy; Aunt Sheila's Uncle Fred. Oh yes, and Aunt Winnie Haggett the dear soul."

All the family has to take turns talking with mother and marvel at the new technology arriving in Leading Tickles.

Shirley reminds me that she now has two guardian Angels –
Dummy Fred and Uncle Henry Ward.

It is December, 1976 and we are down in the Tickle to help celebrate my parents 50th Wedding Anniversary. The usual decora-
tions are hung in the new school auditorium/gymnasium and
excitement and anticipation are in the air. The banquet hall is overflowing with guests. It seems that all the Tickle have turned out for
the celebration. My parents are dressed in their finest threads and
could be mistaken for a couple reaching the golden age rather than
their golden anniversary. It's so good to see so many smiling faces
and well wishers. The Tickle is beginning to come into its own both
socially and economically.

Close friends of mine, like George and Helen Evans, and George
and Clarissa Hiscock, have travelled from Conception Bay South
for this occasion.

George Evans is the Master of ceremonies and he tells about a mis-
understanding in procedure. "I tapped my glass to get their attention but it gave the wrong signal. To my pleasant surprise all hands
began tapping their glasses too. Uncle George looked at Aunt Effie
and says, 'They wants us to kiss.' Whereupon, they stood, and Aunt
Effie, a big woman, wrapped her arms around Uncle George and he
disappeared, momentarily, much to the delight and pleasure of the
gathering.

Later I asked Uncle George if he would like to say something. He
reluctantly stood but when he got started he kept the audience in
stitches, while at same time displaying his fifty-year-old tie that he
had worn on their wedding night.

As I gaze upon my parents, looking so happy and jubilant, I find it
difficult to express in words my sense of gratitude for their love for

each other, and their wonderful parenthood to us all those years. What a blessing for which to thank God.

They always loved so much 'The Chronicles of Uncle Mose' on radio. I've decided to recite for them one of their favorites.

Smoke Room On The Kyle

Tall are the tales that fishermen tell when summer's work is done
Of fish they've caught, of birds they've shot, of crazy risks they've run.
But never did a fisherman tell a tale, so tall by half a mile,
As Grandpa Walcott told that night in the smokeroom on the Kyle.

With 'baccy smoke from twenty pipes, the atmosphere was blue.

Shirley is again busy with the Girl Guides, having taken on the position of Area Commissioner. In 1971 she took on the role of Division Commissioner which extended as far as Conception Harbour. This new position, however, includes Conception Bay South, Avondale, Mount Pearl, and the Southern Shore to Trepassey. She has formed guiding in Avondale, St. Thomas and Paradise, Renews and Ferryland, and re-activated guiding in Conception Harbour and Harbour Main. I don't know where she's getting the energy because she seems to be gone every night with her Guide uniform on.

Debra is also busy as a Girl Guide, as well as a member of the Conception Bay South Concert Band. Mr. Herbert Helen, Supervisor of Music with the Conception Bay South School Board, has put together quite a band. Debbie plays the flute. She and I are also getting more time for discussions about school and the wonderful world out there.

As we slide into the late '70s I feel gladdened by what the school, under the Principalship of David Carmichael, has accomplished and the fact that so many people have made so many contributions to its well-being. Many teachers have come and gone, but they will not forget Queen Elizabeth High with its unique character of purpose, its friendly atmosphere and warm reception, and a body of students that make you feel at home.

Each year new students enter the halls of Queen Elizabeth for the first time, a little bit shy and passive in approach, only to graduate three years later, well seasoned with confidence and hope for the future.

They go to take their places in a world that welcomes them, a world that needs them because they have so much to offer. They have been trained to stand on principle and adhere to their Alma Mater.

David Jones, a well learned Pioneer and President of the Student Council writes, "Every time a Pioneer stands up for an ideal or acts to improve the lot of others, or strikes out against injustice, he sends forth a tiny ripple of hope, and crossing each other form a million different centers of pioneer energy and daring, these ripples build a current that can sweep down the mightiest walls of oppression and resistance. And so with history as our final judge and clear conscience our only sure reward, we go forth to lead the land we love, asking His help and His Blessing but knowing that here on earth God's work must truly be our own."

Heather Chaytor pays tribute to her beloved Queen Elizabeth High. As Valedictorian of 1978, she writes, "From the timid awkward stages of grade nine through the passive carefree years of grade ten; we were students of this school, but not until we reached grade

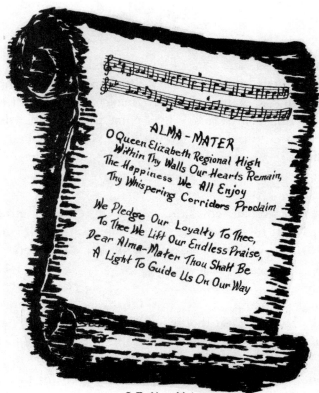

Q.E. Alma Mater

eleven did we realize what a great school she really was... For over the past three years we have laughed, cried, prayed, and cheered together... Together we made up the character of Queen Elizabeth Regional High School: Sharon Porter's interest, Greg Warford's talent, Lori Leonard's happiness, and Gordon Billard's school spirit were well known to us all. There was Harold Porter, the most spirited debater in all Canada, Nancy Lear, a model of determination and a friend to all... Yes everyone of us have had the privilege of leaving our footprints in the lifestyle of Queen Elizabeth."

CHAPTER 8

The Labrador Connection

In 1955 Shirley's mother married Charles Thoms of Irish town, Carbonear. Skipper Charl, as I always address him, is the salt of the earth, a great provider, and a strong believer in his Christian faith. Mother Thoms and the Skipper brought together two families of seven children and then the eighth child, Allan, arrived in the second marriage bonding the family. Even though Shirley had already left home and was married she always refers to the Skipper as Pop Thoms and he refers to her as daughter Shirley. A lot of love and respect between the two have grown over the years. The Skipper,

Mother Linda and Skipper Charles Thoms (circum 1975)

Mother Thoms, Shirley and I enjoy each others company with a good game of Auction. Mother Thoms never wants to lose the game, thus a strategy between the Skipper and myself, ensuring that we have the upper hand. Over the years Shirley and I made many visits and enjoy family life to the fullest.

Skipper Charl spent sixty-three summers fishing on the coast of Labrador in a place called Petty Harbour near Fox Harbour. He had his first summer fishing with his father back before the first world war. He continued his odyssey almost every summer and looked with anticipation to the trip on the steamer with his family as well as a good harvest of cod fish and salmon. This summer of 1978, because of his illness, he had to stay behind in Carbonear and reflect on summers gone by.

The Skipper told me many times about his voyages. Some summers were bumper trips while others were lean. But through it all the trip each summer became part of his livelihood, his heritage, his culture and his very being. To miss it was to uproot his very soul. He and his family would be called 'stationers' since he had his own premises in Petty Harbour as well as his boats and fishing gear. He also took along with him, most times, one to three shareman to help with the cod traps and fishing gear. A shareman was a member of a fishing crew who received and agreed on a proportion of the profits of a voyage rather than wages.

Mother Thoms and daughters, Bertha, Sybil and Charlotte helped with the household chores as well as the fish making. His sons John, Roland and Winston and later Allan made up a fine crew. Mother Thoms told me she used to make a batch (nine loaves) of bread every day and two on Saturday since Sunday was a day of rest from fishing, and a quiet day for reflection. Many a time I listen to the skipper's yarns about summers gone by, cod traps full of fish and the time when Uncle Johnny Curl or Uncle Sol came to visit. We always looked forward to plenty of fish and bakeapples in the fall.

Roland, the skipper's second oldest son left the fishing way of life behind and joined the Royal Canadian Mounted Police in 1957. He later took up Cattle Ranching in Lytton, British Columbia. I asked him to tell about his experiences on the Labrador. Here is his story.

"The *Kyle* is coming." These are the words we longed to hear around the end of May every year. The message was usually delivered via CBC radio out of St. John's and once the word was out it was time to pack the boxes and barrels with every kind of utensil imaginable for us in Petty Harbour for the next six months or so. Items I recall were medical supplies, bandages, ointment, liniment and anything supposedly helpful in curing cuts and sores such as water pops. A pop was a type of boil associated with severe chaffing on the neck and wrists from the rubber pants and jackets incapacitating the men at times. Everything was "home cure." There were no doctors or nurses available so basic medical supples were important.

Needless to say, the thrill of this aspect of the 'big move' was the chance to be the driver of the outfit. All kids loved to drive a horse and cart and sometimes some pretty fancy maneuvers were made on the way to the wharf. Sometimes the horse looked puzzled. As soon as everything was loaded the *Kyle* gave a couple of blasts of her horn, the lines were dropped and we were on our way. People on the wharf and people on the ship would wave and cheer and laugh and cry as we pulled away and headed north. It was very exciting.

Usually, the trip "down to the Labrador" took about two to three days. Accommodation on the boat was very poor, especially for the fishermen and their families who just didn't have the finances to go first class. The steerage, a below-deck room equipped with a long table and maybe 50-100 double tiered bunks, was available on a first come, first served basis. At the top of the gangway the washrooms were located. Everyone seemed to hang out in that area and it wasn't long before the toilets were plugged solid. People were flushing everything down the drain – paper towels, pages of magazines, cigarette packages, etc. It was a stinky mess in a short time. The stewards just couldn't keep them operating. Pails and many other containers became the order of the day; and night, too.

For the men the forward hole was their place of abode for their trip. Usually the hole was filled beyond capacity with freight of all descriptions and quite often there was only crawl space for movement. It was a huge, dark area with three or four 40W bulbs lighting the place. Men were sleeping on boxes, barrels, bundles of fish nets and anything to which they could attach themselves. Many people had no place to sleep. This area was also our dining room for the trip. Imagine, if you can, the atmosphere present in this place, especially as a dining area. The stench from about forty to fifty human bodies were bad but couple it with the smell of the cargo, and a new perfume was in the making.

After being on the *Kyle* for several days, and I remember one trip that took two weeks, some of us were pretty short of sleep. Stan Clarke from Victoria was one of them. He hadn't slept in days and looked like a zombie (sorry Stan). We gave him one of our nesting spots and he slept for about eighteen hours. Not only did he sleep, but he slept balled up on his knees with his rear end high in the air; not surprisingly he survived.

Although conditions were, to say the least, a little lacking, the guests of the "Chateau Forward Hole" were in good spirits. I recall, one evening hearing a rhythmic tapping on the deck beside the forward hatch accompanied by a harmonica belting out the "Stack-of-Barley." "Time to investigate," says I. Up I go two rungs at a time and there is Tom Mercer from Upper Gullies "laying her down." He was a good dancer and a good player. It was great to see and Tom had a good audience.

In the steerage things were not quite so pleasant. Almost everyone was seasick and the kids were having a real bad time. The smell in that overcrowded place was unbearable, crying and moaning were everywhere and the only relief would be the end of the voyage. That happy occasion did eventually arrive and we were all happy to see the rugged coast of Labrador again. A good catch would solve everyone's problem. This trip would be forgotten for awhile but only for awhile. Events like this make life interesting, joyful and sad. They're the core of our being. The events mentioned in this little episode occurred around 1950 and they are as fresh in my memory as if they just happened recently. Many of the people on the Kyle at the time are no longer involved in the fishing industry; many are no longer with us. Fishing families whose names I recall are: Butts, Penneys, Earles, Laings, Forwards, Rossiters, Curls and many more. They were all hard working people with one purpose in mind - providing for their families. They did that but sometimes just barely.

This story depicts one side of traveling on the *Kyle* or any other CN boat on the Labrador run. There are many good stories to be told about those ships as well. I enjoyed every trip. It was all a big adventure to me and my friends. The world was our oyster. We partook thereof.

Cooks, sharemen, and codfish, an unlikely mix, but for six months of the year they were part o f a sometimes poorly oiled machine. I'll deal with the women first. Excluding my mother (Marjorie Thoms (Forward), daughter of Skipper Del Forward who fished in Spear Harbour.) who was too busy raising a young family to become involved in the "hands on" activities of the fishery, all the other women mentioned spent long hours helping with "putting away" the daily catch. Our mother died in 1945 and for a number of years after that we had a different chief cook and bottle washer.

Aunt Rit Kirby, from Flat Rock, Carbonear was our housekeeper for four or five years and she truly was a wonderful lady. She looked after household chores all day long and then when the boys came in with the evening haul of fish she spent hours in the stage heading codfish. She was a strong robust woman and could keep any two splitters going full speed til the birds came home. She did this in cramped quarters (low roof) and extremely poor lighting supplied by a kerosene torch. By the end of the shift everyone was black. Sometimes we were red with blood from mosquito bites as well. It was tough going, especially for the women but they worked side-by side with the men without complaining. Spreading the fish for drying was another phase of the fishery where the women were extremely helpful. After the fish had been cleaned and salted for several weeks it had to be cleaned again to remove the accumulation of dirt and slime that builds up on the fish while in "salt bulk". This term applies to the process of salting and piling the fish to allow the brine to penetrate the fish to add to its flavour and the curing process. Once cleaned, the fish had to be spread on flakes of various descriptions to allow the sun and wind to reduce moisture content before selling the fish to the various merchants. The women played a big role in this whole process. The mosquitos, sand flies and wasps also had their input.

Sharemen came from all walks of life and ranged in age from fifteen to fifty years of age. They were hired by the fishermen to perform whatever duties might be requested of them. Some were humorous, some were cranky, and some always young at heart. Ambrose Williams was one of those. He was about 26-28 years of age but he seemed to gravitate towards the teenagers. He found amusement in just about everything. We called him Am. I decided to play a joke on Am. One day I saw him going to the toilet and in view of the fact that I has just made myself a water squirter from a section of bamboo pole, I figured I'd have some fun. Our toilet was not a conventional toilet. It consisted of a loose plank in the floor of the stage; remove it and you had your toilet. At low tide you could worm underneath the stage and have a perfect view of the toilet hole and the user as well. The secret was to be quiet. Am was already in position and it was a full moon for sure. I crept into position, took deadly aim on Am's behind, and pushed the plunger on my cannon. "KERSPLASH" I hit him dead center - no need for toilet paper this time. I took care of that quite nicely. I expected to hear Am holler and shout and make all kinds of threats, not that it would have mattered, because I was bent over in silent laughter, unable to speak and not too eager to identify myself, at least not until Am had cooled down. However, Am said nothing. He pulled on his long Johns in about half a second and was out of the stage as if he was chased by a demon. At least his leaving gave me the opportunity to breath again and release the laughter that had my stomach in a knot. The disappointing part of the incident was that he never did say a word about the incident - not to me or anyone else. It didn't matter, I had a good laugh then, and every time I saw Am after that I'd have a good chuckle. I wondered if he continued to use the same toilet. Would you?

In Feb. 1955 my father remarried a fine woman and old friend, Linda Clarke of Carbonear. Linda was the widow of Jim Clarke who was killed in a construction accident in Toronto. Linda had three daughters: Shirley , the oldest and then Sybil and Charlotte. To the best of my knowledge Shilrey never graced the shores of Labrador. Sybil and Charlotte did leave their marks in Petty Harbour, and a few marks on me as well. Between them and my sister Bertha, they harassed me beyond words. But I was strong and devious, and in one way or another I made them pay for their cruelty to me. I remember one time I picked up Sybil carried her to a little pond behind the house and plunged her into the icy water. I had peace for a few hours after that.

One nice summer day I was roaming around the hills and I ran across a hornet nest. On the way I met Am. I told him about the nest and right now he wanted to see it. I said, "sure, it's just over the hill; I'll show you the spot." I couldn't understand why he wanted to see a bee's nest. I sure got our of there quickly when I found it.

I was about 200 feet from the nest when I heard Am hollering and cursing. He was running towards me swinging his arms around his face and going through the craziest movements I'd ever seen. I could have sworn he was walking on hot coals and trying to fly at the same time. I was moving pretty good myself, and the bees weren't bothering me. By the time we got back to the house Am was a pitiful sight. His eyes were swollen almost closed, his nose and his right cheek blended as one, and his lip was so badly swollen he could hardly speak. He really was a sorrowful sight. I was almost afraid to laugh but I just couldn't control myself. Oh well, boys will be boys.

The K-Q was a salmon collector boat owned by Earles Freighting Services from Carbonear. They had a business in Battle Harbour, Labrador. Periodically, the boat would stop at Petty Harbour to deliver supplies and pick up fresh salmon. The K-Q carried a crew of two and was quite likely powered by a twin cylinder diesel motor. She also carried a small punt for emergency purposes. She arrived at Petty Harbour one morning in the summer of 1956 heading for Spear Hr and vicinity on her regular run. The crew was John Rumbolt and Hayward Spearing, both in their early twenties. Before departing the boys invited my sister, Bertha and step -sister Sybil to go along for the ride. It turned out to be a short ride. The wind was from the south and quite strong when they departed. As the boat was approaching the headland of Petty Harbour light it developed a bad leak. Water began pouring into the hold and it was obvious that it was sinking. The boys launched the punt over the side and with considerable difficulty, because of the strong wind and choppy water, all four of them boarded the small craft. The boys' seamanship proved its worth in the next couple of hours as they maneuvered the small boat through the breaking waves on the port quarter and at any minute the boat could be swamped- one minute riding the crest of the wave, the next careening down the crest into a churning trough, twisting and turning at the mercy of a turbulent ocean. After a terrifying ride that lasted about two hours they reached hauling Cove. Once around Hauling Cove Point they were sheltered from the storm.

They landed in the cove, climbed some very steep rock bluff to the high ground and after two or three more hours of swamps, brambles and mounds made it to Petty Harbour, safe and sound. Those boys brought that tiny craft through extremely rough seas, completely exposed to the North Atlantic and a strong southerly gale. The boat was heavily overloaded and it was nothing short of a miracle that they survived. Strangely enough, one of the young men involved subsequently drowned in an accident at Fox Harbour.

Experiences such as these were not unusual in those days. Today they would be headlines and the boys would be honoured for their heroism, and rightly so.

CHAPTER 9

Family Ties

This year of 1980, our daughter, Debra, is graduating, with her many friends, many of whom have visited us at our home and in my office. They don't always come to my office for any thing in particular, just to lighten up my day and to see how alert I am to the movements, activities, and thinking of teens today. So I have to try to keep abreast of what really is going on out there in the teen-age world.

When some of them are visiting our home I can't help but overhear: who's going out with whom, why those two broke up, the latest song hit, the Romeo out there, and the chatter goes on.

They have added a great deal to my understanding of the teen world and their many delights, joys, and yes, their problems.

Shirley and I wonder what we will do to catch up with the latest teen activity when Debra is gone from our midst. She has kept us on our toes, but she has been our pride and inspiration.

It has been, and still is, most interesting tracking the graduates of Queen Elizabeth High, after they have gone their separate ways. There is hardly a town or area in the Province or a city in the nation, indeed, a country in the world that one can go without bumping into someone who reaches out his or her hand and greets, "Hi! Remember me, I'm from QE. You were my teacher or

Guidance Counselor; say hello to Mr. Crewe, Mr. Evans, Mr. Best; oh yes, and Mr. Morgan, for me.

Shirley and I were walking through Sherway Mall in Toronto one day and I see this guy hurriedly climbing down a tall ladder with his white coveralls on and a paint can in his hand. He walks towards us with his hand extended, "Hi Mr Parsons, I'm Greg from QE, you were my Guidance Counselor. It's wonderful to see you." And the paint can is lodged down and the conversation goes on.

We were driving through the State of Massachusetts one summer and decided to have a restaurant break. As we walked toward the restaurant a young lady steps up her stride and asks "Are you Mr. Parsons, who teaches at QE?"

"Yes . You are a graduate?"

"No, I'm from Nova Scotia but My husband is a QE grad and he says you were his Guidance Counselor; he's a Gosse from Paradise. So he comes in the restaurant and our ten minute break turns into an half hour. A delightful chat.

I could go on, but suffice it to say that these graduates are everywhere, carrying their warm and friendly smile that is so much a part of their Alma Mater.

It is 1981 and the School for the Deaf in St. John's has been recommending to my brother, Ron and his wife, Tootsie, to send their six year old son, a deaf mute, to the school. This is a normal recommendation, based on a variety of assessments. The parents support it but that doesn't make the decision any easier.

Although I'm Cecil's uncle and also support the school's recommendation I empathize with the parents on their strong feelings of anxiety, and the dreaded times of separation that so many parents go through on decisions and situations of this magnitude. Shirley and I have volunteered to be stand- in parents for Cecil to help make the transition and adjustment a little easier.

The school is housed in Torbay, in one of the old army barricks. Again Shirley prepares herself to run interference, when called, and be there, at least in the initial stages of his young life. On Fridays she, sometimes, picks him up and brings him to his second home, and to embrace him when his longing for his own home becomes overpowering.

Our daughter, Debra, has shown a very positive attitude toward Cecil and is helping him adjust, assisting him with his homework; and Cecil is responding.

Cecil is fast becoming one of the family. Communication was a bit awkward at first but he is so well along with the A S L (American Sign Language) and lip reading, he is teaching us to sign and we are enjoying it.

On weekend visits to his home, bus travel, sometimes, become testy. His mother told me a little while ago of one incident about which she was concerned but, at the same time she was amused. She said the children left on the school bus to be dropped off along the way, in his case Gander. The bus broke down around the park and alternate arrangements had to be made to get them to their destinations. She said they came to Gander and no Cecil. They waited and finally they saw him arriving in this big Department of Highways dump truck, sitting up in the cab as large as life, beside this big friendly driver, eating his favourite sandwich. And then she laughed, knowing that Cecil was being looked after, even under make-shift circumstances.

Cecil Jr. and Katrina, 1981

Cecil and our old English sheep dog, Katrina, have developed a close relationship. Today we are giving her a bath in the bathtub. Many of you, I'm sure, have given your little dog a bath. It's another story with a big dog, covered with wool, a dog with paws that can cover your face, that doesn't want to get in the bathtub in the first place. Thank God it's as gentle as a lamb.

Cecil and I are washing her but I don't have her bath towel. So I sign to Cecil to keep her there, after all it's only a few seconds while I dash to the closet. When I return Katrina has her two front paws out over the bath, securely glued to the floor, the hind paws in the bath. Cecil is in a fit of laughter.

So I coax, encourage, and threaten but to no avail. I try lifting but with her weight soaked in water, and her psychological pull, I give up. Then I hear Debra's voice coming in the house, and she takes off running through the hall with water flying in all directions.

She has never been allowed to come in our bedroom after we go to bed but now that she has charge of the house anything goes. I awaken about three this morning and sense that there are more than two of us in the bedroom. I focus my eyes and staring back at me are those two huge eyes, watching me sleep. I reach out and she stretches full length on the floor, content to be my protector and friend, to the death.

Two years ago after our second pet cat died Debra was so distraught she cried for two days and nights. So here I was down in the back yard with the dug grave, ready for the burial. And then I looked up and both Debra and Shirley were so wet with tears I labored under the loss. When It was over, I promised Debra she could chose whatever pet she wanted as a substitute. The sheep dog became the selection. Need I say more.

The years are passing and Cecil has become an old pro at his comings and goings back home and to our home. He has, very much, become one of the family.

We have been rewarded over and over as stand-in parents. We talk about, with joy, our association with the school administration and teachers at the School for the Deaf, our association with the school moms and their outstanding job in caring for those children who stay in residence. We talk about the activities eg. concerts which we attended and Cecil's participation; the parent-teacher meetings and the good feelings elevating from these. Indeed, good feelings all over!

It's April, 1983 and I've not long returned from the picket lines at Queen Elizabeth High. The teachers have been on strike for a few days and at the moment a settlement doesn't look good.

Shirley advised me that a lady had visited our home in the afternoon and brought a basket of fruit and other goodies. She had expressed concern about our welfare, since the teachers were on strike, and wanted to help. We talk about this beautiful gesture of kindness, even though it was not necessary. How can you measure the goodness and thoughtfulness of people like that.

The phone rings and my dear mother is calling. After exchanging our usual pleasantries she says, "Cecil, my dear, I'm concerned about you and your family with the teachers on strike and all."

"We are fine, mom, you don't have to worry."

"Yes but you must be finding it rough going now that you have no money coming in."

"Mom, don't you worry, we are O.K."

"Why don't you take Shirley and Debra and come down and stay with us. I'll pay for your gas, as well."

Out of all the letters and phone calls I had received over the years, all the love expressed and helping situations covered, this latter presentation of concern reached down to my soul and caused me to want to get in the car and drive down there immediately, not for help, but to get my arms around her and thank God for all the mothers (and fathers) like her.

CHAPTER 10

A New Beginning

Again we are witnessing change at the end of this school year 1982-83. The grade eleven students who would normally graduate are staying for another year, to be the first grade twelve graduates. Mr. Fred Rowe, Principal, is moving on to greener pastures and is being replaced by Mr. Richard Harvey.

Mr. George Evans, a long time teacher, and vice-principal of Queen Elizabeth, is retiring. The students and teachers in their dedication, say this: For almost forty years before his retirement, George Evans has been more than a fine educator. He has served his fellow man in diverse capacities as a drama director in Channel, as a cadet leader in Foxtrap, as a library board member in Manuels, as a P.T.A. president in Long Pond, as executive member in several N.T.A. locals, as an active blood donor, and even as the local "doctor and lawyer" in Plum Point! We students and staff of Queen Elizabeth sincerely thank you, George, for your contributions as an educator, a parent, a citizen and a human being. We also wish you a healthy, productive retirement."

Mr. Evans has fond memories of Queen Elizabeth graduates over the years. Here are two of his stories that he has submitted. "Toss a pebble into the ocean and you have no way of knowing where the ripples stop. It was a beautiful snowy February afternoon. My wife was on her way home from a shopping trip in St. John's. As she approached our post office she decided she might as well stop and pick up the mail. Parking at the post office was at a premium, so she decided to park on the side of the highway. She eased her way in the parking not wanting to go too close to the snow clogged ditch. But alas! That feeling as she felt her car slide where it wasn't meant to. While muddling over how she was going to get back on the road, and before she went to get the mail, a car carrying several teenagers drew up behind her, and out jumped the lads. This caused her some concern. But before she had much time to show concern, one of the lads approached with a sing-song tone of voice "Have no fear, Mrs. Evans, the boys are here." Former students of mine on their way home from university classes had sized up the situation, and recognizing my wife soon had her safely back on the highway."

I don't believe this! I can't believe this happened...

"My wife's cousin and his wife were visiting Central Newfoundland and expressed an interest in visiting St. John's. We extended an invitation to come when they were ready to be our guests. "One small problem", they said, "we have another couple with us." We replied, "No problem at all. You four come on your convenience." They eventually arrived. We took them on a tour of the city, showing off the sites they expressed an interest in seeing. The male non-relative was to meet a friend of his from Ontario who was on a business trip in St. John's. We dropped our visitor off at the Avalon Mall. He waited some two hours at the Mall and his friend did not show. He decided to call us to come for him, when he realized he did not know our names. "Well. I'll just have to thumb a ride." Off he trotted to the highway, stuck out his thumb, and before he knew it a car stopped to offer him a lift. "Where are you going?" they asked. "I don't know." he replied. "Who are you staying with?" they probed. "I don't know. I know we came in over this highway, and that several communities ahead of us I'm staying with a family, his name I think, is George and I believe he's a teacher. "He noticed the car occupants looking at each other and their smiles. This caused him some concern as he was one and they were four. He was surprised, but suspicious, at their next words, "Don't worry. We know where you're going, and where you're staying." This Ontario young man could not get over his good fortune when he was dropped off at my driveway. In the ensuing days, he kept shaking his head in disbelief former students of mine, now university students, had come to his rescue."

In the 1983-84 year the grade nines stay back in the Junior High for the first time since Queen Elizabeth High opened in 1954. The faculty has increased to thirty eight and the number of students is on the rise.

The pioneer hockey team, with many championships under their belt, and under the capable leadership of David Burry and Lloyd Johnson, head off to Kingston Ontario, to engage in friendly competition. Yes, the pride of Queen Elizabeth is abounding.

Educational travel and tours are becoming the thing. Our students travel to educational forums, Open House Canada and, lately, European Tours. Mr. Rice writes: "Learning is no longer equated with time behind the desk. Thus the rationale for travel." He points out that it is difficult to put into words, sometimes, what is expressed in feelings. He continues, "How does one measure the look of awe as a person gazes at David's 'Coronation of Napoleon'? .... 'How does one share the tears of Beaumont Hamel shed by a group of young people for another generation as young as themselves.' Profound thoughts indeed!

Yes, what was considered extensive travel, back in the early sixties, for example, from Foxtrap to Corner Brook, now has become commonplace. Trips abroad – trips to Ottawa, to the various provinces on exchange, and even to Paris are increasing in number.

The school has another long time educator and contributor retiring in the person of George Hiscock. For the past twenty five years George has made a great contribution to Queen Elizabeth High and its well-being. Besides educating the students, in a skilled and professional manner, intrusted to his care, he was always there offering his services in other capacities such as extra-curricula. In the community George is not found wanting, always there ready to help. He has been C.O. of the Church Lads Brigade, Past President and Charter Member of the Conception Bay Lions Club, a member of the local representative council, various positions in his church entrusted to his care, to name a few.

George also taught school in Stone's Cove, Coomb's Cove, Mouse Island and Channel before coming to Queen Elizabeth High. Here is the school's dedication.

"It is both ironic, and perhaps fitting, that George Hiscock, who is retiring this year, should have dedicated to him, a yearbook that marks the beginning of a new era in education in this province. We students of Queen Elizabeth hope that this year also marks the beginning of an enjoyable retirement."

The theme of the first reorganized high school graduating class is "THE FINAL STEPS OF YOUTH." Robin Martin, as valedictorian, says, "When you think of Queen Elizabeth High in the future, draw upon the spirit and concern of understanding in which our lessons were taught, and upon the spirit and love we got from those who were taught alongside of us." A very capable leader, indeed! And his words were not lost to those coming behind for they did "remember the past" and set goals for their year and the future.

Not only did they aspire to scholastic achievements but added extra activities such as the Modeling Club, Rocket Club, Radio Club, Dance Club, Broomball Team, and the French Club.

Trips abroad are becoming more frequent, in the Nation and in Europe. Our students are on the march.

The Guidance department has come fully into its own. Students are seeking help not only for programs and vocational choices but also for personal enhancement.

Our school programs today are so diversified that some of our students look for guidance in the process. Today, the student, more than ever is wrestling with the big picture – what is the best curricula to learn now for the long term. They are no longer satisfied with just a program, and just a graduation, but one that will be most beneficial in the future.

Students are bombarded today with a multiplicity of careers, and many of those complex within its own domain. Then they are faced with specifics within its own specialization. In many cases all they need is someone to lend an ear since the average student spends more time in school than ever before. Time is on their side but they still need to sit and talk about it.

Growing up today is no longer simple and straight forward. Personal problems are many and quite often complex even though we, as adults, sometimes shrug off their questions and concerns as not so important. Some issues that play havoc with their well-being may appear as a passing stage to adults.

The need for the counsellor in the school has been proven over and over, and not just in the high school but in most educational settings. In 1969 when a guidance counsellor was placed at Queen Elizabeth High, part of his time was spent at the Junior High doing counselling, as well as doing periodic psychological testing for special education programs. Today we have an educational psychologist in the system, and a counsellor in each of the junior and senior schools. This year the board has placed an educational therapist at

Queen Elizabeth High to assist in the total process.

Today, as well, students are more tuned to the idea of 'students helping students.' Of course it is correct to say that peers always helped peers and that they make good sounding bases. We do find, however, that formalized peer guidance lends to group approaches as well as individual direction. In the past three years we have increased our number on the peer guidance committee in order to reach out more to the general body of students.

News From Home

It's May, 1986, at 7:00 in the morning and I've just awaken from sleep after an exhausting week-end visiting Lions Clubs. The phone rings and I reach for it. The voice is that of my sister- in- law, Tootsie, "Cecil, the news is not good; your mom has flied away; your mother has passed away. She died suddenly of a heart attack."

I sit on the edge of the bed embracing Shirley, trying to fathom the depths of my loss - my mother, the one that had expressed and demonstrated unconditional love all these years, the mom that taught us to pray at her knee (now I lay me down to sleep), the one that held us when we had nightmares, the one that mended our socks and our hurts, and the mom who worried about us long after we had left home.

Yes, my mother was my contact, my liaison, with the 'Tickle' all these years. She kept me informed of the people and the happenings. From 1950 to 1974, the year of the phone installation in the Tickle, I received approximately two hundred and fifty letters from her, after that, the phone calls replaced the letters. The memories of those wonderful years will live on forever.

Mom and Dad nearing their 60th Wedding Anniversary(1986) with Granddaughter Rhonda graduating.

CHAPTER 11

We Serve

"At the end of the day when you are alone and you know you heard a call for help and you answered it - then you know in your heart the true reward of Lionism." I've quoted these words a number of times this year; I think they were said by Lion Bert Mason.

It's the last week in June, 1986 and Shirley and I are getting ready to go to New Orleans, Louisiana to represent the Lions District of 41-S2, which is made up of 57 Lions clubs, including Gander and the eastern part of the province. As District Governor for the past twelve months, I had to visit each individual club, and meet with those good people who are doing great humanitarian services of helping others. It would take many hours and a lot of writing to tell about all the great moments, rich experiences, human emotions, social gatherings and just plain laughs. At charter nights we were piped in, escorted in, but most times we took our seats in a normal fashion. The governor was introduced informally, formally, seriously and strangely. Lion Jim Combden, Deputy District Governor introduced the Governor at Badger's Quay in this unique way.

Lion Chairman, By the jumpin' dying... we are sure pleased to have the skipper here the nite... pleased as can be... no doubt about it... Now some of you knows the skipper and some of you don't... I s'pose some of you young fellers never laid eyes on 'en before, or behind fer that matter... he's the Top Cat... King Lion... always on the prowl from club to club. Now, he comes from CBS... not a cable channel... Conception Bay South... I was there one time in schooner with a load of Robin Hood Flour... starm of wind too... had to tie up on the Narth side... That lovely woman there with the Governor is Shirley his lovely wife... .take your eyes off her, Lion Bob... she's the lady who tears open his mail... gives him encouragement, and travels witen all the time, I tink... Well the Governor is yer the nite... and tis not every day ye can have a Governor in yer midst... I can promise ye that... .so ye fellers better behave or be haved out...watch yer mouth... no blaggard... .you too Gunner... and if he wants yer woman fer a dance, heave her along... I hope he likes the grub... but I tink he's puttin in a few pounds... he'll dance em off later. We're some glad to have ya yer Skipper... along wit ya lovely bit a stock... come again any time... yer always welcomed... mark that down...

We anticipate what it will be like at the International Convention because we have already gone through it, a year ago at Dallas, Texas, where approximately one hundred and eighty countries of the world were represented, where dozens of languages were spoken, where many cultures were displayed, and where different skin colors, creeds and dress were evident. There was, however, one overriding factor that bound us together, and that was the Lions emblem, the lapel pin with the motto - 'WE SERVE.'

We sat with six hundred and sixty District Governors from all over the world, shook hands with some, greeted others in our native language, didn't understand the words sometimes, but smiled, knowing full well that we had a common cause- that of serving mankind.

In 1973 Lion Heber Best invited me to join the Conception Bay Lions Club which was formed in 1971. This is a service organization, committed to doing good things for people less fortunate, and with emphasis on the humanitarian acts of kindness. It has been a pleasure working and socializing with so many caring people in

Conception Bay South and, indeed, in the great Lions District of 41-S2.

Over the past thirteen years I have witnessed so many acts of kindness, undertaken by groups of people banded together for a common cause. Many people outside service organizations have faint ideas of what those members are doing, but one has to feel a part of the action to get caught up in the 'helping others' climate. For me the experience has been enlightening and uplifting..

The International President's motto for this year has been, 'We serve better together' and that is something we have proven over and over. Within the Lions Organization a group can take on a service project to enhance the cause that cannot be done alone.

On the district level fifty seven lions clubs can take on projects that cannot be done by one club. And one and a half million lions and thousands of lionesses, on the international level, can take on major service projects and realize outstanding results. We know because lions have done it. Lions have spearheaded blindness to help prevent it as well as correct it. They have taken up the fight against diabetes. They have helped the less fortunate in their educational, vocational and humanitarian needs.

Yes, it is great to be a Lion! And here are some extracts that I've repeated many times this past year. As I ponder the state of Lionism in District 41-S2 this year, I wonder what some communities ever did without it. When I read that a cerebral palsy victim, Wendy, had been helped to no end, when I read that Benny has been taken care of, and that Jennifer had been sent to Children's Hospital in Toronto, supported by lions, then I know all is well.

When I know that a typewriter has been donated to a blind and handicapped person, a wheel chair to the Red Cross, special eye glasses to Little Luke, then I know all is well.

When I read that many clubs are supporting Boy Scouts, cadet movements, etc. and that the child who couldn't afford the uniform, received one; and that a child's final wish is granted, then I know that all is well.

When I know that most of our Lions Clubs are giving to the Lion Max Simms Memorial Camp, that caters to diabetic children, the disabled, blind, disadvantaged, then I know all is well.

How proud Lion Max Simms would be today, knowing that the camp that bears his name, is doing those great humanitarian activities. For even though he was a great lion he was first and foremost a great humanitarian, committed to a deep sense of human worth. Despite the loss of both legs and the sight in one eye, he still had the will to share the vision of service.

Fellow Lions, Lionesses and Leos, you help the youth, the senior citizens, you give assistance to third world countries, you help at home and abroad, you stand behind the 'We Serve' emblem, and look great in the eyes of the recipient, because you are great.

I salute you, fellow Lions, as great humanitarians – people who care about others and have the desire to help those in need- need of the basic necessities of life, need of friends, need of encouragement, need of knowing that they are never fighting life's battle alone.

My year is all but finished, not as a lion, but as District Governor, and I have to thank the cabinet and the general Lions population, approximately seventeen hundred in 41-S2, for your help and support . It has been overwhelming.

My Principal, Richard Harvey, and School Superintendent, William Lee, went out of their way to accommodate me this year. They, too, know the tremendous service that Lions are doing world-wide; and more than that they are tuned in to the local service that the lions are doing in our community.

Despite Shirley's poor health this year, having been stricken with a heart attack and gone through by-pass surgery, she has been the one that has kept me going, when things got rough. After all she had a successful year as District Lioness President back in 1982-83 at which tine I had to chase her around while she visited all the Lioness clubs in the district. I cannot put it into words better than Lion Jim Combden of Badgers Quay who has already penned his thoughts about Shirley.

Shirley - 1986

TO SHIRLEY

You were always there,
a lantern to the feet of your Captain
who with firm and steady hand
guided the Lions ship, with its proudly flying flag
into distant ports
where the hand of service was extended to
— the widow
—the handicapped
—the diabetic
—the drug user
—the lonely and forsaken.
You the mate with calm and tranquil disposition,
gave confidence to the Captain,
when fog enveloped the harbour;
when storms delayed departure;

when troops deserted.
Even the doctor could not keep you from sailing;
for your love for the captain
exceed your fear of the sea.
Shirley, you and the Governor, our Governor,
the lion who guided us with superior skill and ability,
do serve better together;
and when the last port is served,
you will return from the sea
to rest—
to reflect—
and to record your memoirs in a golden scrapbook.

CHAPTER 12

Graduation – Queen Elizabeth High Style

For twenty-six years I've had the privilege of attending sports awards nights, dances, remembrance day services, and other special occasions. No gathering has had such a profound effect on me, and I'm sure, on other teachers, as the graduation ceremonies.

Each one, each year, seems to take on a special meaning of its own. Graduates seem to have become more aware of the sensitivity of it all and they make it a very personal moment in their lives. And it is a very special time - a time of mixed emotions and final 'good byes.'

I shall take the last four years as examples of students pouring all their hearts and energy into the preparation of graduation ceremonies. The common denominator are theme songs that give voice and music to their reflection of the past, celebration of the present, and hope for the future.

First the grad prom with all its grandeur - the well decorated cars in the motorcade, the graduates dressed in formal ware - tuxedos, split tails, white dinner jackets, bow ties, evening gowns of all descriptions, hair styles galore, manicures to match the decorum. Wow!

They are off to the hotel with horns honking and lights flashing.

"Tonight is our night of royalty
Just take a look around
We are symbolic of our future
Success is where we are bound"

At the hotel the guessing goes on. "No, that can't be Kim; yes, it is; look at her beautiful gown."

"Who is Shawn escorting? Oh, that's Cindy."

They all look so wonderful in their formal attire. The teachers are having a hard time recognizing some of the students that were in their classes yesterday.

"We celebrate the end but it's really just the start;
We've come so far together and I'll hold you in my heart;
We can move into the future with the strength
            that's in our past;
We'll face the world with courage 'cause our dreams
            were born to last."

After the elaborate meal, salutations and speeches, the students intermingle, exchange greetings, admire each others style of thread and glamour, and dance to the latest jazz and other music.

Is this the beginning of another 'Jump Off' on the road of life, or 'A Question Mark in Time.'

"Questions Marks in Time
We can't really know
Whether time will make us strangers
Or time will make us grow !"

Approximately five months later the two hundred or more graduates parade into the auditorium of Queen Elizabeth Regional High

School to the music of the Conception Bay South Concert Band under its director, Miss Margaret Rowe. Each person is dressed in his/her cap and gown, and they are here to receive their diplomas, certificates, and awards. They greet each other, after a short absence, but realize full well that tonight is really their last time together as a group. When they toss their hats high, it is a finality of sorts.

> My friends, for you I will keep a special place
> I will now say a silent good-bye
> Rest well in your designated space
> Once more, my friend, good bye.

The valedictorians, Susan, Robert, Todd and Andrea, of the last four years emphasize to those graduating with them that they should not lose sight of the past and particularly Queen Elizabeth High which helped to shape who they are. They referred to the pleasant and exciting high school years and the valuable lessons taught for new beginnings.

CHAPTER 13

Moving On

It's June, 1987 and our daughter Debra has made the announcement, "I'll book my flight to Toronto to look for work.' Her friend, Janet, has already gone; her friends, Butch, David and Colleen are also up there, and others as well.

Debra has already graduated from Memorial University. She is, as well, working on a job but not in line with her training. Word has it, according to her, the chances of getting work in Toronto is greater than in our Province. So that's what it comes down to for many of our young people. If you want a job in line with your training and a better pay check, leave Newfoundland.

This 'going away' is not something new, nor is it unexpected. Over the last number of years I've been listening to parents who have attended parent-teacher meetings and other gatherings, tell their stories of their sons and daughters leaving home. Some parents are resigned to it while others still lament those moments of separation.

Of course, when we look at it in another way, what a blessing it is to live in a country like Canada, and be able to travel from one province to another, and say proudly, 'I am a Canadian. I can go where the jobs are, and I can go back to my province to visit, to stay 'a spell' and reminisce about my growing up and my school days in Island Harbour, Lewisporte, Gambo or at Queen Elizabeth High, Foxtrap.'

Still it doesn't make 'going away' any easier. We just got back from the airport after waving good- bye to our daughter, knowing full well that this is the beginning of another phase in our family life - one of physical separation from those you love.

Our voices seem to echo off the walls, her room feels lonesome. Even our old English sheep dog, Katrina, senses her permanent absence and lays her paws over her face to block out the silence.

"It's September, and I'm standing before my thirty- three charges in Island Harbour one room school. I look at the range of my students from beginner to grade VIII, with two senior students in grade X and I ponder how I'm going to apply my six weeks of teacher training to this real classroom setting. Questions keep running through my mind. Will I start with the beginners or will I go first to the senior students setting for C.H.E (Council of Higher Education)?"

Thirty-EIGHT years have gone by since that first day in the one room school – that first day when I felt so alone and home-sick, and not sure if I was on the right path or not.

Peer Guidance Assistants 1988

As my mind stretches back into the past, I remember so many helping images that assisted me on my journey that has helped me to
arrive at this stage – the stage where I'm getting ready to retire and
leave Queen Elizabeth after twenty-seven years. I know I will miss
her whispering halls and the youthful faces of her students. But it's
time to go and make room for fresh thinking in the guidance
department and a younger counselor to whom the students can better relate.

The speech night ceremonies are always formal and exciting, and
help students realize the end of one part of their journey, and the
beginning of new paths. I have the honour of addressing them at
their formal gathering.

'I can't help but stand here in admiration as I gaze over such an
important gathering of the community – a gathering made up of
great minds, intellect, and great models of society. Besides all the
other greats – school board, school officials, I look down here and
I see my colleagues with whom I had taught, some as long as
twenty-six years. It was a pleasure to have had that association. We
have been fortunate to have gathered so much knowledge, training
and caring, all in one school.

I move further down the isle and I see friends everywhere – no
strangers. I see parents that were my students, grandparents that
were my students. And even now as we meet in the supermarkets,
in the malls, or along life's way, we chat and reminisce of days gone
by, and some will say, "I bet you don't know me now." And I will
reply, "I bet I do," and our thoughts of the past become paramount
to the present. The time has passed and we have arrived at this
stage. We reach across and up here with our hearts and our love to
the most important people here tonight your sons and daughters,
and our students.

As parents, you wonder how you ever reared them because you
reflect on the time that your five year old son came home from

school and stated emphatically that he didn't like the teacher and would be a kindergarten drop-out. In September you convinced him that he should go back, and he declared he might try it for one more year.

And you recall how your six year old daughter announced that she was leaving home, so she packed her doll's suitcase and proceeded to the gate, hoping you would call after her and you didn't; and you were hoping that she wouldn't go any further and she didn't.

Remember the very first time you brought your boyfriend home and mother warned your father not to say anything – anything – and he did! And things have never been the same since.

Thirteen years of schooling have shot by and you sit there all beautiful in your caps and gowns. We are very proud of you and your accomplishments. You are our reason for being here and making our lives more meaningful and worthwhile. I congratulate you on your achievements and scholarship. It was an outstanding year at Queen Elizabeth High. Treasure the memories.

I could give you all kinds of statistics: where the jobs are, what pays the most money, how to make your first million, how to get a date with the girl of your dream. That, however, is not my purpose. You may very well be confused as it is, at this stage. That is not so bad either because out of confusion quite often comes a stronger commitment for where you want to go and what you want to do. Those of us who fail to attain our goal or who have less success than expected, very seldom use their full potential. Seek out the true meaning of life and its self-worth and use it as a foundation to combat stumbling blocks. Set aside blame and move along with a positive attitude, using your God given talents and intellect fully and wisely. And Karen will go on to become the medical doctor, and Toby the fine arts specialist, and Joanne the caring nurse. Each of you will realize your dream, that with carefully thought-out and wise decisions will become a reality. Try to avoid climbing the ladder too quickly, especially at the expense of others. Always be sensitive to the needs of others and with your strong foundation, you will find the true meaning of life. 'We are like ships in the night, we pass, wave, and sail into the darkness, sometimes never to meet again. But the splendor of lights, and the magnificence of sails connect our hearts and minds long after we have disappeared over the horizon.'

I want to recite a poem composed by James Combden, a school teacher at Badgers Quay, especially for young people like you and he has kindly given me permission to use it.

HUMAN SHIPS

Tonight you lie, anchored in port,
Ready to cast off;
Your lights are burning brightly now,
The wind – inviting – soft !

Your lights the harbour sets on fire,
Its rays do circle 'round;
And you, the captain of your life,
Prepared and outward bound.

O' lights so bright, from whence they come!
To guide you as you roam;
In search of peace and joy and love.
That light, friend, came from home.

From mom and dad with values strong,
Implanted all those years;
With care, compassion, patience deep,
Occasionally some tears.
The brilliant light upon the mast,

Doth knowledge symbolize;
To guide and help you wisely choose,
Your handsome girls and boys.

And in your school your light was born,
Your teachers helped it glow;
So don't forget when far at sea,
Your teachers and your school.

Your ships, lit up with many lights,
Around the rails of birch;
Your faith so strong like a mighty tide,
A gift from a solid church.

And so I look upon you now,
Already to set sail;
With lights aglow and sails all trimmed,
I know you cannot fail.

So let your light shine in the world,
Sprinkle your rays around;
And with your eyes upon the stars,
You'll never go aground.

Now, as you push off from the pier,
We wish you peace and joy;
Go forth to serve your fellow man,
From Queen Elizabeth High!

CHAPTER 14

A Garden Wedding

It's June, 1994 and we are in Mississauga, Ontario, attending our daughter's wedding. There is a lot of excitement in the air as we make ready for the big day.

I feel certain that most of us have heard the argument that if you are going to get married you should go to your church, exchange your vows, because God is present there. He will sanctify your marriage and make everything right. We have also heard the good news that God is present everywhere if we wish Him to be so.

Our daughter, Debra, grew up in the Anglican church, whereas her fiancee, Gary Nagle was raised in the Roman Catholic church. They both, decide they would like to have a garden wedding but they want an ordained priest from one of their denominations to perform the ceremony. After some asking around they are told that regulations forbade the priest or minister in question to carry out the marriage outside the church building.

They approach a United Church Minister and he tells them he would gladly perform the ceremony in the garden. An added bonus is that he is a Newfoundlander, ministering in Ontario. Debra and Gary are living in Mississauga.

The day is set and the happy couple are hoping for a sunny day so that the open air ceremony can be perfect. Gary called the Pearson Airport weather office a couple of times to an update on the local weather. One lady at the office must have sensed his denominational upbringing because she suggested that he should hang a string of rosary beads on the clothes line to ensure that the weather goes right. The garden is chosen – green pasture, carpet green lawns, a variety of trees. Butter flies are busy moving from flower to flower, squirrels and chipmunks move in secret places, and a variety of birds sing their songs of love. A little church in Marysville is chosen as an alternate to exchange their vows in case of rain.

The cast is set. The guests are in their places, seated under the beautiful blue sky, with over-hanging apple blossoms for shade and fragrance. The two violinists, playing classical music, switch to 'Ode to Joy' as Debra and her dad slowly make their way up the green pasture toward the modest cloaked minister. "Dearly beloved, we have come together in the sight of God and..."

I can hear the minister's words and then I behold our daughter and about-to-be husband standing there in the sight of God, and in the presence of their families, friends, and nature at its finest. The birds are now moving ceremoniously in chants, a chipmunk peers down from the top of a tree, and a cow is heard to moo,moo on the neighbours's farm next door. "I now pronounce you husband and wife, together, in the name of the Father, and of the Son..."

I feel certain that God did bless them with His love as well as sealing their love for each other.

Debra and Gary's Wedding1994

CHAPTER 15

Our Youth - A Positive Force

A Dialogue

SCENE ONE

The stage is set. Aunt Maggie, Aunt Sissie and Aunt Emmie, all seniors, meet at least once a week to have a cup of tea and discuss the latest happenings and 'going ons' in the community and abroad. Aunt Maggie is about to pour the tea.

Maggie: Have you been reading the paper lately, Sis? You know the youngsters is going to the dogs. See where the three teens stole the van and drove it until it ran out of gas. One of them was thirteen years old. Out gallivanting and traipsing around the roads all night long ! Another crowd stole a car on Bay Street last night. The rod is what they need... my dear, if I owned 'em.

Sissie: Yes Meg, I read about it. The police said they think it's the same ones doing it. What would a thirteen year old be doing out that hour of the night? Where are the parents in all of this? But Meg, wasn't that nice, about that service club, I think it's called the Kiwanis Club that looks after the music festival. Did you see the pictures of the children singing on television? How many atoll must be involved... and the schools... and the teachers... how many children must be trying out back in the schools? What opportunities the children have today?

Meg: Yes, well. And that poor girl in the convenience store the other night must have got some fright. Two of the youngsters, that's all you can call 'em, sixteen and seventeen years old, went in with socks over their heads and had a knife. Took whatever money was in the till. What bold faces, my dear! They must be on drugs to do the like of that. The police got 'em but they can't name 'em. Young offenders, my dear, young offenders.

Sissie: Meg, did you ever attend one of those speak-outs for children that the lions club has on the go? I was up to the Lions Club the other night listening to those young people speak about various topics. My granddaughter was involved. It would do your heart good to listen to them. What training: three from Holy Spirit and three from Queen Elizabeth High School. Imagine all the children trying out for something like that back in the schools. I was up to St. Edwards School last spring listening to the grades three to six children taking part in their oratorical. They say all the elementary schools in the area take part in speaking out. You know they stand on their feet and speak to an audience.

Emmy: Isn't that wonderful. I have a granddaughter that took part in the Junior Speak-out. You know, Sis, they had eight students speak at the Lions Club. There were four from Villanova Junior High and four from Frank Roberts Junior High. They were delightful. I could have listened to them all night. And the entertainment they had when the judges were out. What singing by those young girls! Meg, did you take part in public speaking when you went to school?

Meg: My dear, if we said anything when we went to school the master would let us have it in the gob. Did you hear what happened down on Archer's Street last night? A fifteen year old maiden decided to have a few friends in for a party. The crowd that's always swarming around the streets got wind of the party, went up and forced their way in .... fifty or sixty of them...... smashed things, a lot of damage. On the dope again, I daresay.

Siss: I heard that on the radio this morning. They said there were about ten of them and maybe the same crowd. Meg, my dear, I was down to Holy Spirit School to the cabaret last night. What a time and performance. Have you ever attended one of them? The young people do some job; must be dozens of them; and the bands are playing, and the children singing. It was a musical, of course.

Meg: Another grandchild of yours, I s'pose. Have another cup of tea?

Siss: I don't think I'll have any more. I have to go down and drive my grandson to the hall. It seems there is a group of them who get together and do volunteer work, helping the seniors and shut-ins. My dear, Jimmy comes home telling about all the wonderful things they do. He seems so happy doing it. Thanks for the cup of tea.

SCENE TWO

An afternoon tea at Aunt Siss's

Meg: I was reading one of the Mainland papers yesterday and on the front page was this headline. 'Regional police look for teen muggers who robbed three people waiting for the bus.' Imagine youngsters being muggers. They took their jackets, money, and even the shoes off their feet. They can't be named. Merciful glory, what's the world coming to atoll?

Emma: Oh that must have been the Mississauga news. I saw that; made the front page. Further in the back of the paper was another headline which read: KIDS AND VOLUNTEERING: A WINNING COMBINATION. What a heart warming story. It was from News Canada. They were talking about how kids can beat boredom by becoming involved and learning leadership skills, building self-confidence, gaining valuable experience, and making a real difference in people's lives. What was that again? Oh yes, Canada's National Survey on volunteering said kids accounted for more than 150,000 volunteer hours in the year. My dear, the children of today have so much energy and know-how; they can make circles around us.

Sissy: Well! You know, Emmy, it's the same thing here on the island. Look at all the children that pitched in for the Tsumani Relief. How many children took the leadership, even in the elementary schools; and they gave their pennies. Heartwarming, it is, heartwarming.

Meg: Yes, Sis maid, I've been thinking about what you said the other day. We never seem to get any of the good news on the front page of the papers, or hear much about it on open line or...

Emma: You know, Meg, more children would be involved if the parents encouraged them and got them teamed up with friends.

Sissy: Some of the teens who are not involved said they would, if they were asked. And you know, older children love working with young ones, and seniors, and animals. They would like to get involved.

Meg: Maybe we should attend more of those performances by the young people that the schools have. We'll probably see them in a different light. I must ask my grand son, Johnny, if he's involved in other things besides study.

Emma: Sis, I think I'll try a piece of that apple tart. What say we all get ready after supper and go to the little concert St. George's School is putting off. It's for parents, but sure we are all grandparents and there's plenty of room. Exit

Children, today, live in a very complex society. They turn on the television, and the world, with all its good and evil, comes flooding into the living room. Geographical documentaries, world leader profiles, technological advances, medical break-through, and the latest fads catch their attention. Reports on terrorist attacks, suicide bombings, information on strange and new viruses and diseases, and the catastrophes resulting from tidal waves and earthquakes play havoc with their sense of security.

They access the internet on their computer and are helped by a wealth of information and resource material. They are also confronted with gutter E-mail, pornographic material and a great deal of unacceptable material and images. They haven't left home yet and may already be bombarded. Thanks to responsible parents they may be spared the onslaught of negative information on the internet.

And then they are off to school where learning continues; where, again, choices have to be made with the help of trained teachers, guidance counselors and administrative officials. Peer pressure is prevalent. Thank goodness, some of it is good. How well the child can avoid the 'not so good' will depend immensely on wise parenting and well trained school personnel

Some teens are off to supervised community activities, while others experiment with street ventures, and test whatever lies in their path. Most youth make appropriate decisions and fall into an 'acceptable order of living.'

If, forty years ago, one asked a teen what kind of a career he would chose, all the traditional vocations would come flooding to mind... teacher, fireman, nurse, doctor, plumber, etc. Today they are not only faced with literally hundreds of classifications but with a multiplicity of variables within each category. But yet through all these challenges they fare extremely well. The small percentage of children who demonstrate unacceptable behaviour manage to steal the front page of most newspapers. Is it any wonder that Aunt Maggie would think the 'youngsters are gone to the dogs?'

For many years I've viewed, and interviewed the youth, with most of it being done in educational settings. I've witnessed their being put down, have listened to their being praised and elevated to great heights. Most are survivors, accepting praise and constructive criticism. They move with the flow.

All children require the basic needs of living. Most of them in our developed countries have those needs. Many, as well, need a lot of understanding and love to off-set the anxiety, depression and stress that accompany obstacles in life.

Like I said before our children fare well, given the pressures they face. But parents need to be vigilant. All children need to be listened to, not just the words. Listen to their feelings. Listen to all they have to say. Rejoice with your child when he has success. It may be raising his grade from 50 percent to 60 percent. Show you are really happy.

As well, show concern when he is not performing. Most good parents will need to know the cause, and rightly so. To be a good parent one doesn't have to be book- knowledged. A good parent takes responsibility for his child, shows more than a passing interest in his activities. They protect them, but not smother them. They discipline them but not abuse them. They give them safe freedom but know when to rein them in. And they allow them latitude but not at the expense or inconvenience of others.

I had the privilege of interviewing officials at the two local high schools about our youth as they perceive them today. My first interview was with Scott Crocker, Principal of Holy Spirit School which has an enrollment of 746 students. He said that about twelve of them are problem children who lose a lot of time from school primarily because of home problems. He has been principal for four years there and during that time he has seen no fights or violence. He said schools today are better with more facilities, and more children are staying in school, therefore more problems. He does worry about some children getting into drugs and alcohol on week-ends because there is more liquor available and it's easy to get. Mr. Crocker advises the parents to focus on the positive things in their children' lives rather than the negative. His concluding statement, "Even though life is more challenging in school today, we are in good hands with our youth. Leaders will naturally come to the front."

My second interview was with Derek Stevenson, guidance counsellor, at Queen Elizabeth High for the past seventeen years. He said children today are no worse behaviorally than they were fifteen years ago. They are better informed and more knowledgeable today because they have greater access to more information. But they are quite capable of sorting things out and ninety percent of them choose wisely. Some of the other ten percent take up much of the school's time dealing with unacceptable behaviour. Some of them lose too much time from school due to personal problems that affect them but that are beyond their control. None of the students are really bad; they just need more guidance and direction from both home and school.

I asked Wayne Rodgers, the Principal of Queen Elizabeth High what he thought of the old saying, "The youngsters are gone to the dogs." He expressed the feeling that the saying has been with us for a long time and will continue to be used by young adults and seniors alike. Every older generation thinks that the generation coming behind them present more problems or perform more deviant acts of behaviour. All agreed that the media do emphasize the negative in youth and pay less attention to the positive things that students do.

Here are just a few of the volunteer activities that students are involved with at Holy Spirit High: guidance assistants, interact junior rotary club, student council, and school council. Many also take leadership courses on juvenile diabetes, and MS. Some senior students also give support to primary grade children at Topsail Elementary in French, as well as in skating.

At Queen Elizabeth High students are involved, as well, in many programs. Here are a few of them: guidance assistants, Tutoring for Tuition, SADD (Students Against Drunk Driving), yellow ribbon campaign (program for suicide intervention), safe and caring schools initiatives, Kick the Nic program and 'helping in the community' program. The Mentoring Program really caught my ear. Michelle Clements, Vice-Principal at Queen Elizabeth explained to me how it works. She said the school has some senior students who go to Upper Gullies Elementary after their own school day is finished to meet primary grade students, one on one. They tell social behaviour stories through activities such as puzzles and crafts. The objective is for the small child to get positive bonding with older students who are role models. One of the senior students who has been a representative in drug awareness has assisted the police in their presentations on the drug program.

When I listen to teachers, administrators and guidance counsellors tell about all the activities in which students are involved I can't help but feel a swell of satisfaction. Not only are many of them involved but they do a fine job in their roles as leaders and performers. Needless to say we do have a positive force for good in our youth. Maybe they should be allowed to take over the responsibilities of running the affairs of the province and the country. They would probably develop more peaceful and agreeable solutions to the problems at hand.

CHAPTER 16

Lionism

"It will not matter whether we (Lions) are curing blindness, educating a child, digging a well, or building a park, because everything we do will be in harmony with our essential role in the world," said International President Kjit Habanananda in 1999. He was emphasizing the need for all levels of lions, from international to club level, to be in harmony with each other.

In 1971 a group of community minded citizens of Conception Bay South met to consider the needs of the community and ways to meet those needs. After discussions with Lion District Governor Stuart Toope, it was decided to form a local Lions club. Thus began an organized service that has had far-reaching results for the good of the community.

The Lions Club took the initiative and supported the construction of the Conception Bay South Stadium. The club also donated the land and pledged $100,000 towards the Conception Bay South swimming pool complex.

The many services which the local Lions Club has provided are numerous. Contributions to Conception Bay South Fire station, Victorian Order of Nurses, school playgrounds, Scout troops, food banks, Literary Council, Janeway Telethon, and sports organizations are some of the many endeavors that the Lions Club has supported. Humanitarian projects are many.

My involvement with the Lions Organization over the past thirty two years has done wonders for me. Like many other lions, I have given hundreds of hours of service to the cause "We Serve." However, it hasn't been all giving. I have received much that has given me a fuller life and helped make me a whole person. I have been given the opportunity and privilege to see first hand what Lionism is doing throughout the world. I have witnessed the satisfaction on the faces of givers and the appreciation in the eyes of the receivers.

My involvement in volunteer services has also helped me to realize that a selfish approach to life is not a healthy one. The material things we strive for are not so important after all. The inconveniences we experience seem to fade in importance as we witness the smile and satisfaction on the face of a child helped through the Children's Wish Foundation. What about the feeling of satisfaction one gets when witnessing the joy on the face of a person in a third world country who has just received her sight after cataract surgery. Those examples of humanitarian service help one to realize that life can be more pleasant if we do something for someone every day, even a phone call or a visit.

Most of the Lions Clubs of District 41S2 do similar services as the Conception Bay South Club. Lion Rita Pennell of Trepassey does her walk through the community for the Janeway Telethon. Here is the beautiful image of response. As she walks by the houses the residents leave their homes and walk to the highway to meet her, sharing their gifts of love for the Janeway Hospital and the children that it serves.

St. John's Health Care Lions make pillows for cancer patients. Badgers Quay Lions canvas homes to get blood donors in case of emergency at the Hospital. Grand Bank Lions raise money for families of marine disasters. Services vary from club to club and indeed from country to country yet they are all united by one major idea

"We Serve."

In 1983 the Lions Foundation of Canada was founded and its first project was Canine Vision Canada. Shirley and I have twice visited this fine facility in Oakville, Ontario and have toured the training area. This school trains dogs for challenged individuals, the blind and hearing impaired. It allows these people to live independently.

In 1986 a number of lions stood in the terminal at Gander International Airport and welcomed Lion Cec Curtis and his guide dog, Gunner, as they disembarked from the plane, making the moment a significant one for the lions family of Newfoundland and Labrador.

In February, 2004 at a District Governors Organization Meeting in St. John's the Lions had the opportunity to observe these dogs in action. The seeing-eye dog, the hearing-ear dog, and the special skills dog (for those with physical or medical challenges) are truly amazing.

At the International level Lions support Lions Clubs International Foundation which provides disaster relief around the world. Because Lions International has no political or religious affiliation it is accepted in all countries regardless of political structure or religious beliefs

To show the reader how the services of lions vary from country to country I shall quote Governor Azariah Oram. "At the International Convention in Detroit, Michigan, I met people from all cultures and from many different countries. We met a couple from Zimbabwe who told us they are no longer able to care for AIDS patients because all their resources are being used to care for the children left behind when both parents have died of aids. My friend from Croatia told us about the period during the recent war in their country and explained their program to teach children not to step on land mines. At an International Convention I met some Lions from Indonesia where Lions have made a difference in relief efforts during the recent Tsunami. Lions are accepted by even the most repressive regimes as they know that they are there simply to serve others in the best way they can."

How many times have we heard the line 'But I'm too old to join an organization or help at the community fair; after all I'm over sixty and I've done my part over the years." A few days ago I heard this story. The word went out from a community church that they needed a group to come to the hall on Saturday to do a special project for needy families. An eighty- six year old lady turned up at the hall. The leader of the project suggested that maybe Aunt Maggie should sit and take a 'spell.' Aunt Maggie was not impressed. "Young lady" says she, "I'll be sitting around long enough when I get old. Now where shall we start?"

The Lions District of 41-S2 takes in much of the Eastern part of the Province and spear-heads large projects of it own, financially supported, for the most part, by the clubs. Projects such as the District Speak-out, and Diabetes Awareness are on the priority list but I feel the greatest project ever undertaken is the Lion Max Simms Memorial Camp, located in the Bishops Falls area. The camp was a dream of Lions Jiggs Borland of Bishops Falls Lions Club and A. Jack Baker of the Botwood Lions Club. They were the two, supported by many other lions, who initiated the project and did the ground work. A debt of gratitude is owed to them and to all the great lions who assisted to make this project a reality. The complex is designed in pod form and can accommodate approximately eighty over-night patrons. It has a swimming pool, a recreation room, a health room and an expansive lounge. The camp is financed primarily by all the Lions of Newfoundland and Labrador. Over the years most of the clubs have given generously of their funds to sustain the Camp and its facilities. Sometimes individual lions or people that support the lions movement standout in fund-raising. The fund raiser that caught my attention was the SQUID MONEY raised by PGD Clayton Sansome. According to Past District Governor Phil Field, Lion Clayton had a business in Hilgrade, New World Island where he used to collect squid from the fishermen. When the camp was being built Lion Clayton sold part of his squid quota for the camp and turned over the proceeds to the camp building committee. Hence the name 'squid money.'

There were also the Lioness Clubs (formerly called Lionettes) of Newfoundland and Labrador who gave of their time and money to support the Camp. Of course, they also supported dozens of other projects on the district level as well as those in their own local clubs. Most of their activities were 'hands on' and of a humanitarian focus.

This Camp is the facility that bonds the two Lions Districts – 41-S1 and 41-S2 together and is a source of pride for all lions because of its great service to human kind. The camp serves literally hundreds of disabled and disadvantaged people each summer and receives a lot of praise and thanks for it efforts. Let us take the camp for the mentally challenged. They are received with a air of independence and given the freedom that they rightfully deserve. They dance, swing, play games, swim and go on boat rides. They go back home with enough to talk about for the rest of the year.

The same thing may be said for the diabetic children. They learn to gain a greater sense of independence and have a great time doing it. Administering their own needles, checking ones sugar count, learning from each other what foods affect their diets, become commonplace among the campers.

The lions of Newfoundland and Labrador are proud of this fine facility and continue to finance it year after year because the camp is doing what lions want it to do – bring a feeling of well-being to those children and put a smile on their faces.

Shirley and I had the privilege of attending the sod turning ceremony for the camp back in 1978. In 1981 the camp was officially
opened and Lion Philip Field of the Mount Pearl Lions Club
became the first official Chairman of the Lion Max Simms
Memorial Camp Foundation. Lion Phil just celebrated fifty years in
lionism and what a fine story that could make, as told by a great
lion. Indeed, a great humanitarian! Lion Phil has been a member in
three Lions clubs – St. John's, Grand Falls, and now Mount Pearl.
He has adhered, with steadfast devotion, to the motto, 'WE
SERVE.' If you ask Lion Phil about Lionism, and more especially
about the Lion Max Simms Memorial Camp, he will relate stories
of compassion, caring and giving with the same enthusiasm that he
has displayed for fifty years. Now that's devotion and service!

Mention was made earlier of Past District Governor A. Jack Baker,
and his role he played in the origin of the Lion Max Simms Camp.
Lion A. Jack, as he was respectfully called, shouldered the camp and
ran with its fund-raising. He wrote letters of encouragement, of
financial need, of good deeds, about the camp. He composed and
sang songs about the camp, and loved it when the cheques rolled in.
He kept his finger on the camp and reminded clubs when they were
slack with their donations. Here is a verse of A. Jack's Theme Song
about the need to continue to support the camp

BRINGING IN OUR CHEQUES
Tune–Bringing in the Sheaves

Working in the morning, working in the evening,
Thinking of our target for the Max Simms Camp
Waiting for a letter, sure to come from A. Jack,
Who will be rejoicing if we bring a cheque.

Chorus
>   Bringing in our cheques, bringing in our cheques
>   We shall come rejoicing bringing in our cheques

Lion A. Jack knew how to stir the crowd and to get a positive response. Somewhere in the procedure he would manage to melt down the hearts of lions, lionesses and leos with this song:

THERE ARE KIDS
Tune: There are smiles

There are kids who need a little sunshine,
There are kids who need a week at Camp;
There are those who love the way you do things'
And the help you give to those in need.

There are smiles that make me oh so happy,
There are hugs we share 'tween you and me,
But the things that fill my heart with sunshine,
Are the cheques that you give to me.

Here is a story that will give us food for thought. Lion Jim Combdon sent this extract to me several years ago to insert in my newsletter when I was governor and he has given me permission to reprint it.

The Pride of Newfoundland and Labrador Lions

THE PARABLE OF THE LIONS

About thirty years ago there lived in the jungle animals of different abilities, interests, philosophies, and economic standards. They had one thing in common- they all belonged to the jungle.

As most creatures know, it's dark, very dark in the jungle. Disease, fear, discrimination, hunger and poverty exist in intolerable amounts. The jungle was not a good place to rear young cubs and other species. And many of the lions knew it and wanted to do something about it.

One night a rabbit got caught in a wire snare. He was rushed to the Great Auk Memorial Hospital where Dr. Deer performed a delicate operation. The rabbit's life was saved, but the cost to his family was staggering. There was no insurance. Something had to be done to alleviate the financial burden on the family.

An older lion convened a meeting of his neighbours. Cats, bears, wolves, cougars, owls, deer, moose and others met under an old rotten log. All were curious and wondered what the Senior Lion was up to.

They didn't have long to wait. "We need a mechanism," he began, "to deal with basic animal needs here in the jungle."

No one helps me," sniffed a fat old lynx.

"Some of us are lucky," said the chairman, but the jungle has many very unfortunate souls who need help in one form or another."

A rich lawyer lion asked, "Why do we have to give our time and money to others?"

"Well," continued Leo, "just look around. Don't you see a need to help some animals here? I know, we all know Billy the Beaver will not finish his house before winter sets in. He's old and we should give him a paw, a claw or a foot. It'll be good for our souls too."

"And Mrs. Squirrel, the one whose husband died last week – does she have enough nuts for the winter? She had six kids," added a bull moose.

"Right you are," said black bear. "We should help her. And, Red Fox, the one who got his leg badly damaged in a foreign object last winter? He can't get to the store. He can't shovel snow away from his den, and he's very lonely, hardly ever gets out around anymore. Someone should visit him some time. Probably we should all visit him."

After an hour of discussion, the chairman commented, "It seems to me you're receptive to the idea of some organization working toward the easing of the sufferings of others. Let's vote."

By a vote of 90% they decided to form a club. For some time they debated the name. Wolf pack? No. Rabbit Association? No. Owl Committee? No. "Why don't we call it a Lions Club?" said the only elephant present. "A Lion called this meeting and lions are strong brave creatures." So they settled on Lions Club and everyone went home full of joy and enthusiasm.

For years they laboured in the Auk Jungle which got lighter and lighter as the years passed. Sick birds were visited; bats had their eyes examined; bears were provided with 'stay awake' pills; senior animals were treated to a banquet at Christmas; Red Fox had weekly visitors and Widow Squirrel has more nuts than you could shake a stick at.

The Club raised funds through a sale of fall leaves, a jungle calender depicting all the animals and their birthdays. Every week they raised funds by playing "TAG". It was fun; all the activities were fun, and the fact that they were helping the less fortunate gave the club deep satisfaction.

Years passed and things changed. Some members became too self-centered. Ernie the Elephant devoted full time to his business-making artificial elephant trunks. He rarely attended a meeting. Others lost interest, always making excuses for not doing this and not doing that; in fact 'making excuses' was a big industry in the jungle. And still others just drifted away, and became totally absorbed in their own small world.

At a meeting of the Board of Directors the King Lion, his whiskers twitching in agony, his roar a mere whimper, said, "I'm sad to hear that some of you are thinking about leaving; I'm equally sad to see so many leave the club over the last few years. But I'm proud of the few who have remained through "thick and thin," who did more than your fair share and who, I am sure, will remain faithful to the end.

"I feel we are sending too much money out of the jungle," commented a tall giraffe, who hadn't attended many meetings lately.

Leo the King stroked his whiskers, "Writing cheques is not the only way to serve others," he said. "What about the collection of berries for wine to be dispensed at the Animal Hospital for Children to the young with low blood? I didn't see you tramping through the swamps and over barrens".

The giraffe was silent, the whole body silent.

"Some of you didn't take part in Jungle Animal Welfare Day," added the president. "I was tired, said one Lion. "Two weeks in a row... just too much."

You hunt two weeks in a row," replied Leo. "You tramp through the jungle two weeks in a row. We all do many heavy things two weeks in a row, yes seven days in a row. Feeble excuses and rationalization are not good enough."

"I didn't take part," said one member, "because I had to take my pet canary to the vet."

"We all had something to do," replied a faithful Lion in the back of the den. "My wife wanted me to trim the walkway to our house, but I told her it could wait one more day."

"And I had eggs to paint," added Mr. Bunny.

"And I'm still looking for a place to sleep for the winter," growled an old bear, "but I helped rake the leaves on that special day; and I don't regret it. I still expect to find a place for the winter."

"And I gave a hand," said an old grey squirrel, "and I haven't washed and packaged my nuts for the long cold winter."

"That's true," said the King Lion, "but many of you are not keeping the commitment 'to serve' you made when you joined this club. You have put yourself first. I don't mean your family and your job, but purely selfish interests have come first, and that's why a few have to do the work that should be shared by all."

"The spirit is dying," whispered the oldest Lion in the Club; and I'd say if we lose five or six of our committed members this club could lose its charter." Everyone was silent, for they knew the wisdom of these words.

EPILOG

The club survived. New blood, not much was added, but enough to sustain growth and carry out projects.

Time passed. One by one each Lion died and was buried in the soft jungle turf. The founder died first. Animals came from all over the jungle to pay their last respects. One could tell he'd never be forgotten. In fact a tree was dedicated in his honour and to his memory. As each died, the jungle was filled with moaning and grief. Multi-coloured leaves were sprinkled over each grave which was marked with a jungle stone on which was engraved: "HE LOVED OTHERS; HE GAVE HIS LIFE IN SERVICE." The citizens of the forest did not forget. Their good deeds were often discussed and their graves were frequently visited. They lived on in the hearts of the jungle folk and their lives inspired others to follow in their humanitarian tracks.

Sadly, the others died too. Those who turned their backs on the call 'To Serve' passed away. The former Lion who'd rather fill his own stomach than collect for hungry mouths died peacefully in his sleep one cold foggy night. Few cared, his funeral was not well attended. There were no moans in the jungle. The former Lion who was always too busy to attend meetings found time to die as well. He was buried before most realized he was gone. His grave is somewhere in the jungle, and the member who lived totally onto himself, too selfish to share his blessings with others also fell into a permanent sleep. He left behind the biggest den in the forest. He was not remembered. Not quite true – a civil war was fought over his worldly goods which could have been used to help the needy in the jungle. For the measure of a man is...

THE MEASURE OF A MAN

Not... "How did he die?" But... "How did he live?"
Not... "What did he gain?" But... "What did he give?"
    These are the units to measure the worth
    Of a man as a man, regardless of birth.
Not... "What was his station?" But... "Had he a heart?"
And..."How did he play his God-Given part?"
    Was he ever ready with a word of good cheer,
    To bring back a smile, to banish a tear?"

Not... "What was his church?" Nor... "What was his creed?"
But... "Had he befriended those really in need?"
Not... "What did the sketch in the newspaper say?"
But... "How many were sorry when he passed away?"

– James Combden

Chapter 17

Salmonier Retreat Group

In 1979 a group of fourteen friends decided to organize a trip to Salmonier Line and make it an annual event. Such an outing would take place at the opening of the ice fishing season usually in February. The word went out as to what to call this group. After many submissions we finally settled on 'Salmonier Retreat Group.' First it was a one day activity, then a one day and one night thing . It soon developed into a long week-end from Friday to Sunday. This year we celebrated our twenty-fifth anniversary and charged our glasses to the devoted friendships that can be hard to beat. We still miss Johnny Tibbo who lent a lot of humour to our gatherings.

Let me paint you a picture of a ice fishing week-end by the retreat group. The patrons start arriving at #2 Henders Drive at around 10 AM. By 6 P.M. all have settled in and await a delicious four course meal that the cook and his assistants have prepared. After grace is said or sung and a toast made to friendship and absent friends, we enjoy the meal. A cribbage tournament is ongoing through the week-end. Other games like 500s and a friendly game of poker are available according to ones interest. In between games, current topics of vital concern, e.g. same sex marriage, sponsorship scandal, are given some serious consideration.

A patron's birthday is always acknowledged and the individual toasted. I recall the year when George Hiscock celebrated his sixty fourth birthday; we sang the song 'For now I'm 64' a number of

times on the week-end. A few days afterwards, back home, someone asked me how old George was and my reply was 'I'm not quite
sure.'

After a good night's sleep the cook and his cookees are making
ready breakfast as each patron appears from the dormitory in good
form. Breakfast consist of eggs, bologna, ham, bacon, home-made
bread toasted, with assorted jams – bakeapple, partridgeberry, etc.
At around 9 AM skidoos line up to portage patrons to the nearest
pond where scouts of the group are already there with shelter constructed, dry kindling prepared for fire and some holes bored.
Needless to say a friendly atmosphere has set the stage for a good
day.

The day progresses well with patrons taking turns checking lines for
pan size trout. Pranks are common among the friendly group. I
remember my turn to check the lines and when I try the third one
there is definitely one on, so I am excited and pull it through the
hole displaying it at the same time, only to realize the trout is
already stiff. I suddenly realize that Monty had done the job on me
by hitching one that had already been caught. I can hear the roar
from the make-shift abode. Stories abound around the fire while we
taste the treats, brought by patrons – corned fish, rain-bow trout,
cod tongues, assortment of caplin, kippers and mussels. Monty's
shishkebabs are always a treat. Later in the day some of us move to
another pond to help with the catch.

At the end of Saturday night all competition, e.g. cribbage is complete and discussion of major topics continue until bed time.
Patrons, on Sunday morning, are somewhat somber, realizing the
week-end is far spent and we will soon separate. After the breakfast
is enjoyed there are selected readings from the book (not the good
book), but the diary of poetry composed by Sparkes or Rice. It gives
the group an opportunity to reflect on episodes of past years and
smile a little at our own shenanigans.

Suffice it to say that a week-end at # 2Henders is equivalent to at least two weeks at sunny Florida. At the beginning of our get-together, sleeping quarters was limited and patrons had to sleep heads and tails on the floor. Heber, being the kind and considerate host that he is, added a dormitory to his cottage to accommodate all the boys so that each had his own individual bunk, except for Parsons and Evans who always laid claim to the bridal suite, as Heber coined it.

The catch of trout is usually given to one, two or three sick people in the community with the blessing of the Salmonier Retreat Group.

Salmonier Retreat Group

CHAPTER 18

Relaxing in the Tickle

Each summer we make our way back to Leading Tickles to spend pleasant moments in the "not so old homestead" where we invite friends to come and enjoy the Tickle hospitality and scenes of nature at its finest. We show our friends the 'board and trail walk' that extend from one end of the island to the park – a wilderness trail that have breath-taking scenes of natural beauty. One almost needs to pack a lunch, take a spell along the way and feed the blue jays that await ones treats.

Early morning walks take one to Ocean View Park where icebergs may be viewed, and scenes of spectacular beauty await the visitor along the beaches. Caplin may roll on the beaches, whales may blow nearby, and wild sea birds take their fill of a varied ocean spread.

When we come to the Tickle we become one with the residents. I make my way to Bax Rowsell's store where, at certain times, men gather to exchange the current news or tell stories of days gone by. We visit folks, like Will and Jan and stay for tea. We yarn about days of yesteryear and wonder if we have the story right at the end of the evening. We attend the new and beautiful St. Nicholas Church where we sing hymns of hope and praise, where we pray together, and where we renew our covenant with God. While there I think of my Grandma Susie sitting beside me like we used to many years ago, and I intermingle my thoughts with the past and the present.

New St. Nicholas Church, Leading Tickles

We also attend social gatherings of all descriptions. The largest social event of the year, however, is Leading Tickles Day when the population swells and multiplies many times, when Ocean View

Family Re-union at Ocean View Park.
Menu: Fresh Fried Caplin, Lobster and Fisherman's Brewis.

Park becomes a field of humanity. Pick your choice of foods- cod tongues, cod fish or salmon platters, jiggs dinner, and other delicacies. Strangers and friends come from all over to enjoy the food and friendship that are present in abundance.

Boats of every description are tied to the various wharves. There are long liners, speed boats, cabin cruisers and, once in a while, a schooner boat and a yacht or two. Periodically a coast guard ship ties to the public wharf and enjoys the local hospitality. It seems that people who come, marvel at the scenic landscape and tickles of all descriptions. Solo Sailor Sam Walters stopped at the Tickle on his trip around the island of Newfoundland in his sailing boat, Petite Megan. He said this about the Tickle as quoted in the Western Star, "Leading Tickles is full of small islands with heavy growth trees, with beautiful rock formations. If people ever found out about it, it would be bombed with people."

I have enjoyed many boat rides that would add flavour to any newcomer's visit. Today Cyril Rowsell has invited me for a leisurely cruise in his boat. We leave from Ariel's stage head, motor down through the Tickle, along the fish plant and community stage where fishing boats are busy landing their lobsters, crab, or caplin, depending on what time in the season it is. We pass through under the causeway and head for Northern Tickle, view Tinker Island and Woody Island, and scud along by Bear Cove Head where Uncle Mark used to have his cod trap, years ago. Our conversation becomes more excitable as we reminisce about long ago times, when fish was plentiful and fishing gear marked the shoreline. We head toward Burnt Island Point and the Sunker, where Uncle Arch sometimes dropped his moorings from his trap- skiff, the scow. From there we pass by Western Rock where Uncle Ben and his crew used to winch up by capstan an overload of fish. The surplus fish, of course, was given to extra boats hanging on the head ropes of the cod-trap, waiting for the nod from the skipper.

I look out the bay and imagine seeing Uncle Israel on Uncle Israel's spot, and Uncle George Hannam on deep-water bank, with their killicks or grapnels down, 'lowering her down' with the hook and line or the two claw jigger.

Cyril interrupts my thoughts and says, "Cecil, I have to show you the bald eagle's nest on the back of Burnt Island. I've been keeping an eye on them for a while now. Oh yes, and you must see the carvings of the land that the sea has shaped." So we nudge the boat in to the shore and I stare in wonderment at the forging that only nature can make beautiful. I've forgotten some details but Cyril reminds me that Uncle Israel used to have his salmon net there, and Alf used to have his here, identifying specific points. I'm doing a double take here now because while he's telling me all these things I imagine companies of turrs flying in the bay, and wooden boats, with 'make and brake' engines chugging along shooting at the flocks and collecting their kill. Sling goes the old musket.

"Cecil, Cecil," calls Cyril. We are steaming around Man Point. "Now Cecil," shouts Cyril, "I'm going to land you on the point where your father used to tie on his salmon net." Thank God it's calm today. I recall times when dad used to jump from the boat, with raging seas all around, on to the point in order to attach his surface line. He would say, "Wilson, you get to the paddles to sheave the boat in close; Ron, you get ready to reverse the engine." He never did miss the point and fall in the water. Cyril lands me and I become lost in a sea of yesteryears. I imagine the large Atlantic salmon shining and glistening in the nets. Dad and Uncle George Rowsell's nets run from the land parallel to each other. Sometimes the salmon would be running so well that one would strike the net while one was watching. "Fine sign today," says dad as he rolls a 'big ben' cigarette with a contented look on his face.

I jump aboard Cyril's boat and we steam around Man Point Cove, head in through West Tickle, through the Shoal Tickle and land at the Flake Point on Rowsell's Island. Cyril with that relaxing laugh says, "the goats are coming to meet us. We are going to have a stroll on the island. Too bad we didn't take a lunch." This is the island where father grew up, where Wilson was born, and to which my parents returned year after year, after they left, to set their vegetable patches. I can see mother with the old iron bake pot over the open fire cooking up a feed of fish and brewis or a fresh Atlantic salmon during our visits to the island.

"It's time we head down through the Main Tickle," says Cyril. As the boat skims through the water I see the marks for Newfoundland bank where Ron and I used to spend a lot of time jigging. I see the mussel bed, and the little island where we used to set our lobster pots. As we pass the houses I imagine seeing the elders of days gone by, spreading caplin and codfish on the flakes, and others are pronging cod fish out of the boats upon their stage-heads. Grandma Susie is out on the bank picking up chips to get the old waterloo stove heated. I turn away and come back to reality as the spray from the boat gets in my eye. As Cyril docks the boat at Ariel's wharf, I look overboard and see connors lazily moving along the bottom. Maybe I'll come down after supper and catch a few.

This morning we sit there and eat our breakfast in that same abode, where my parents used to sit, and gaze out on the Tickle where whales entertain us with their frolicing scenes, where long liners go and come with their catches of crab, where the plant and the public wharf are alive with humanity and the activities of making a living.

But more than that the public wharf is a place where men gather and yarn about the present and what really happened yesterday and this morning. But more especially they talk about how things were before the cod moratorium; with many of the elders, before Confederation times.

Yes By'. I minds the times when...

We leave the house and go to Ocean View Park that has become a Paradise of sorts. We get checked in at the main gate and head for Western Bear Cove, where dozens of people congregate to watch the caplin roll on the sandy beach. Sometimes one can see the fins of cod intermingled with the small fry, no doubt having their fill, but not as pronounced as days gone by. Children run the friendly waves, men and boys carry dip-nets to catch the little fish shimmering and dancing on the beach. A pot-head whale hovers close, and nature seems to blend its many colors with the setting sun.

Shirley walks across the long beach to her tranquil place on the other end where she reflects in quiet solitude and speaks of being at one with nature.

Entrance to Ocean View Look-out, Leading Tickles.

I climb up to the look-out and have my spell. First I look out at Bear Cove Head, and Burnt Island Point, Tinker Island and Nose-worthy Cove Point where fishermen of long ago and not so long ago, set their cod traps. It is now a memory.

I gaze across toward Cape St. John and up toward the Mouse Island and down toward Sculpin Island where fishermen used to tend their trawls and gill nets by the dozens, as gulls and gannets and tickleaces circled on souring wings or bobbed near by, waiting for the fall-out.

I see the berths where salmon nets skirted the shores and fishermen picked the prime fish from the mesh and raised the big one high, as onlookers wallowed in admiration.

I think about the landwash littered with remnants of wooden boats that rest from weary voyages of days gone by, ignored and unwant-ed, to sleep forevermore on dry land.

And I look way down over the hill, way down to the cemetery which adjoins the park on one side and the beautiful Eastern Bear Cove on the other, and I know resting there from their life's toil are the remains of our forebearers. They are at peace with the rolling waves, the songs of birds, the smell of fragrances from trees and blooms, and salt sea air.

I close my eyes and become one with nature and the past, until I'm alerted by some voice, "Some view, skipper."

I open my eyes and focus on the young man. "The best," I reply. "Where are you from ?"

"I'm from Toronto, sir, but my grandparents were Rowsells from the Tickle. I just visited their graves and placed some flowers in their memories."

Congratulations

to

Queen Elizabeth Regional

Hgh School

on

her 50 years of

outstanding service

to the cause of education.

ON YOUR WAY, PIONEERS!

After 50 years of wedded bliss it's time to celebrate

Cec and Shirley - 50 years of marriage

and relax

Cec and Shirley - relaxing at home

ABOUT THE AUTHOR

Cecil Parsons was born at Leading Tickles, Notre Dame Bay, Newfoundland. He grew up there, and attended a one-room and later a two-room school, from which he graduated in 1950.

After teaching for one year at Island Harbour, Fogo Island, and two years at Leading Tickles on "C" and "B" licenses, he attended Memorial University where he attained a B.A.(Ed) and a B.A. Later he earned a M.Ed. from the University of New Brunswick in Guidance and Counselling.

Cecil taught school in other communities throughout the province, but 27 of his 35 years were at Queen Elizabeth High School. It was there he taught, primarily, Social Studies, and for the last 20 years served as guidance counsellor to hundreds of high school students.

Cecil and Shirley Clarke, of Carbonear, were married in 1954 and they have one daughter, Debra.